English Phonetics *and* Phonology

English Phonetics
and Phonology

An Introduction

Philip Carr

First published 1999

2 4 6 8 10 9 7 5 3 1

Blackwell Publishers Ltd
108 Cowley Road
Oxford OX4 1JF
UK

Blackwell Publishers Inc.
350 Main Street
Malden, Massachusetts 02148
USA

British Library Cataloguing in Publication Data

A CIP catalogue record for this book is available from the British Library.

Library of Congress Cataloging-in-Publication Data

Carr, Philip, 1953–
English phonetics and phonology : an introduction / Philip Carr.
p. cm.
Includes bibliographical references (p.   ) and index.
ISBN 0–631–19775–3 (hc. : alk. paper). — ISBN 0–631–19776–1 (pbk.
: alk. paper)
1. English language—Phonology. 2. English language—Phonetics.
I. Title.
PE1133.C34 1999
421—dc21   99–19742
                                                                      CIP

Typeset in 10 on 13 pt Palatino
by Graphicraft Limited, Hong Kong
Printed in Great Britain by MPG Books, Bodmin, Cornwall

This book is printed on acid-free paper.

Contents

Contents

Contents

Contents

Preface *for* Teachers

Each year in the Department of English at Newcastle University, I am given eleven 50-minute lecture slots in which to introduce English phonetics and phonology to around a hundred students in the first semester of their first year on a variety of different undergraduate degree programmes, including English language and literature, linguistics, English language, modern languages, music, history and many others. Also included in the student body are European exchange undergraduates and students taking applied linguistics postgraduate degrees in media technology and in linguistics for teachers of English as a second language.

Given the range of degree types, this is a daunting task, made even more difficult by the fact that a substantial minority of the students do not have English as their first language. In a typical year, the student cohort will include speakers of Arabic, French, Spanish, German, Greek, Japanese, Korean, Mandarin or Cantonese Chinese, and Thai. Many of the non-native speakers will have been taught RP; others will have been taught General American. Amongst the native speakers of English, very few of the students will be speakers of RP, so that the non-native speakers are more likely to speak RP than the native speakers.

The vast majority of the student body will take their study of English phonetics and phonology no further, and the one factor which the majority of this diverse band of students shares is that they have no previous knowledge of phonetics or phonology; the course must therefore be *ab initio*.

One faces a dilemma in teaching such a course: on the one hand, one wants to cater to the small minority who will go on to study phonology at a more advanced level. On the other hand, one wants to introduce the subject without overwhelming the students with a mass of bewildering descriptive detail and an avalanche of seemingly arcane theoretical constructs. It is a moot point whether this dilemma can be resolved. However, this textbook was written as an attempt at a solution.

It is arguable that textbooks are harder to write than monographs, and that the more elementary the textbook, the harder it is to write: one can barely write a line without being aware of one's often questionable assumptions, and one has always to resist the temptation to question them in the body of the text. One continually has the sense of one's peers looking over one's shoulder and guffawing at the absurd oversimplifications which one is knowingly committing to print. But it has to be done: students have to learn to walk before they can learn to run; they also have to learn to crawl before they can learn to walk.

Writing and using textbooks is an empirical matter: it is very often immediately apparent when an exercise, chapter or book is simply not working, for a given body of students. Almost all of the textbooks which I have used on the first-year Newcastle course described here have proved to be unsuitable for this type of student cohort in one way or another; mostly, they have contained far too much detail. I have therefore set out to write a very short, very simple coursebook which deliberately ignores a great many descriptive/ theoretical complexities.

My aim has not been to introduce students to phonological theory; rather, I have sought to introduce some of the bare essentials of English phonetics and phonology in a manner that is as theory-neutral as possible. This is fundamentally problematic, of course, since there is no such thing as theory-neutral description. I have therefore decided to adopt various theoretical/descriptive views, such as the tongue-arch/cardinal vowel approach to articulatory description, the phonemic approach to segmental phonology, the trochaic approach to English foot structure, and so on, on the purely pragmatic basis of what I have found to be easiest to convey to the students.

I have ignored acoustic phonetics for the very simple reason that our department lacks a phonetics lab, and I have not included distinctive features, since the mere sight of arrays of features marked with '+' and '–' symbols seems to render large numbers of my first-year students dizzy (particularly those majoring in English literature). I have also excluded feature geometry, the mora, underspecification and a great many other theoretical/descriptive notions, in an attempt to pare the subject down to a bare minimum of these.

The first four chapters are deliberately very short indeed, and contain only the most elementary introduction to articulatory phonetics. My aim there is to offer the student a gentle introduction to the course. I have spread the introduction of the phonemic principle over two chapters, since, in my experience, students find their first encounter with these ideas something of a quantum leap. The chapters on word stress, rhythm, connected speech phenomena and accent variation contain a very stripped-down, minimal, account of those subjects; I hope that there is enough there to act as a foundation for those students who wish to study these matters in more depth. In the chapter on syllable structure, I have been a little more ambitious in introducing analytical complexity, on the assumption that syllable structure is something that beginning students seem to be able to get the hang of more easily than, say, rhythm or intonation.

I believe that one of the most important duties of a university teacher is to encourage, or induce, in the student a sense of critical awareness, a grasp of argumentation and the role of evidence. On the other hand, one has to be very wary of introducing students at the most elementary stage to the idea of competing analyses: they find it difficult enough to get the hang of one sort of analysis, without being asked to assess the merits and demerits of competing analyses (even at the post-elementary stage, most undergraduates are very resistant to the idea of critically comparing different analyses). I have tried to overcome this dilemma by introducing competing analyses and assumptions at one or two points, while consciously ignoring them elsewhere.

The exercises are meant to be discussed at weekly seminar/tutorial meetings; my experience is that, if phonetics/phonology students are not made to do exercises, they easily come to believe that they have grasped the subject when in fact they have not. It is my hope that students who have completed this course would find it possible to tackle more advanced textbook treatments of these topics, such as those given by Giegerich (1992), Kreidler (1989) and Spencer (1996). Whether that hope is fulfilled is, of course, very much an empirical matter.

Preface *for* Students

This is an elementary introduction to English phonetics and phonology, designed for those who have no previous knowledge whatsoever of the subject. It begins with a very elementary introduction to articulatory phonetics, and then proceeds to introduce the student to a very simplified account of some of the main aspects of the phonological structure of present-day English.

It is arguable that there are two main questions one might ask in studying the English language: what is it about English that makes it a language (as opposed to, say, a non-human communication system), and what is it about English that makes it English (as opposed to, say, French or Korean)? This book attempts to provide the beginnings of an answer to both of those questions, with respect to one aspect of English: its phonology.

Thus, although the subject matter of this book is English, there is reference to the phonology of other languages at several points, often in contrastive exercises which are designed to bring out one or more differences between English and another language. These contrastive exercises are included because native speakers of English, who often have little or no detailed knowledge of other languages, tend to assume that the phonology of English is the way it is as a matter of natural fact, a matter of necessity. For many such speakers, it will seem somehow natural, for instance, that the presence of the sound [f] as opposed to [v] functions to signal a difference in meaning (as in *fan* vs *van*). To the English speaker, [f] and [v] will therefore seem easily distinguishable, and that too will appear to be a natural fact. But the fact that these sounds have that function in English is a conventional, not a necessary or natural fact: English need not have been that way, and may not always be that way. Just as one can gain a new perspective on one's own culture by learning about other cultures, so one can gain a fresh perspective on one's native language by learning a little about other languages. One can also, in learning about other cultures, gain some sense of what human cultures are like. Similarly, one can begin to get a sense of what human language phonologies are like by learning in what respects they resemble each other. Those points of resemblance concern general organizational properties of human language phonologies, such as the phonemic principle and the principles of syllable structure.

Reading a textbook on linguistic analysis is not like reading a novel. It is vital that the student complete the exercises at the end of each chapter before proceeding to the next chapter: they are designed to get the student to apply the ideas introduced in the chapter. The reader will not have properly grasped the ideas contained in this, or any other, textbook on phonology by simply sitting back in an armchair and reading the text, even if the student is under the impression of having understood the ideas. Vast numbers of students who have attempted to master linguistic analysis without actually doing it have ended up with disastrous exam results: no one ever became any good at linguistic analysis without actually doing it.

Like most linguistics textbooks, this book is cumulative in nature: what has been introduced in earlier chapters is presupposed in later chapters. It is fatal, therefore, to let several weeks go by without doing the reading and the exercises, in the hope of catching up later: the result is very likely to be that you will simply find yourself out of your depth, even though this is an elementary textbook. It is simply not possible to dip in and out of a linguistic analysis textbook, no matter how basic, in the way that one might dip in and out of a dictionary or an encyclopedia.

This book is designed to cater for students who, in all probability, will not pursue their studies in English phonetics and phonology any further. However, students who will be proceeding to a more advanced level should be able to tackle more advanced textbook treatments of these topics, such as those given by Giegerich and by Spencer (see Suggested Further Reading at the end of the book). Those students should also find it easier to tackle one of the many introductions to general phonological theory which are not focused on English (again, see Suggested Further Reading). In order to prepare such students for more advanced study, I have introduced, at some points, an indication of some of the difficulties with some of the assumptions made in this textbook, or a brief discussion of competing analyses. Although this textbook merely scratches the surface of the subject matter, I hope that there is enough here to make the subject of phonology seem intriguing to the student who intends to pursue his or her studies.

It is my hope that this book will be of some use to teachers of English as a foreign language, although it is not designed specifically for such readers. I am always surprised to discover how little in the way of knowledge of English phonetics and phonology such teachers often have. I have no experience of such teaching, and while I make no suggestions as to how the notions introduced in this book might be put to use in the TEFL classroom, I find it hard to believe that a knowledge of the basics of English phonetics and phonology could fail to be useful to the TEFL teacher in some way, even if only as background knowledge which extends the teacher's knowledge of English. I also hope that some of the contrastive exercises might help suggest ways in which one's native language phonology can interfere with one's attempt to acquire English as a second language.

Acknowledgements

I am grateful to several cohorts of students in the Department of English Literary and Linguistic Studies at Newcastle University whose feedback has been valuable. I am also indebted to Patrick Honeybone, Maria Maza, Irenie Rowley and Charles Prescott, who acted as tutors to my students, and whose comments on several drafts have proved most helpful. Thanks too to my colleague Karen Corrigan, who commented on an early draft. Many years ago, in a small mud house on an island on the White Nile, I introduced James Dickins to the clements of phonetic description. He has kindly reciprocated by supplying me with the Arabic data on p. 51, for which I thank him. I also owe a debt of gratitude to the seven anonymous reviewers of my original proposal for their comments, and to Steve Smith, Mary Riso and Beth Remmes at Blackwell for their patience and encouragement. They may well be surprised that it took so long to write such a short book; I can, however, console myself with the fact that I do not have to offer the (perhaps apocryphal) apology: 'I am sorry this book is so long; I did not have the time to write a shorter one.' Finally, many thanks to Blackwell's reader, Andrew Spencer, whose intelligent, informed and insightful comments on the pre-final draft were immensely helpful. He is not, of course, responsible for any remaining inadequacies in the text.

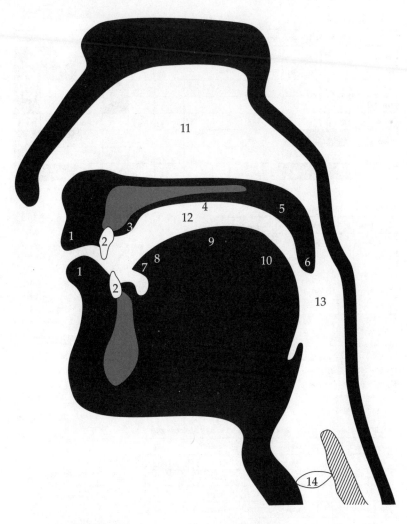

1 Lip
2 Teeth
3 Alveolar ridge
4 Hard palate
5 Soft palate (velum)
6 Uvula
7 Tip of the tongue
8 Blade of the tongue
9 Front of the tongue
10 Back of the tongue
11 Nasal cavity
12 Oral cavity
13 Pharynx
14 Larynx

Figure 1 The organs of speech

CONSONANTS (PULMONIC)

	Bilabial	Labiodental	Dental	Alveolar	Postalveolar	Retroflex	Palatal	Velar	Uvular	Pharyngeal	Glottal
Plosive	p b			t d		ʈ ɖ	c ɟ	k ɡ	q ɢ		ʔ
Nasal	m	ɱ		n		ɳ	ɲ	ŋ	ɴ		
Trill	ʙ			r					ʀ		
Tap or Flap				ɾ		ɽ					
Fricative	ɸ β	f v	θ ð	s z	ʃ ʒ	ʂ ʐ	ç ʝ	x ɣ	χ ʁ	ħ ʕ	h ɦ
Lateral fricative				ɬ ɮ							
Approximant		ʋ		ɹ		ɻ	j	ɰ			
Lateral approximant				l		ɭ	ʎ	ʟ			

Where symbols appear in pairs, the one to the right represents a voiced consonant. Shaded areas denote articulations judged impossible.

CONSONANTS (NON-PULMONIC)

Clicks	Voiced implosives	Ejectives	
ʘ Bilabial	ɓ Bilabial	'	Examples:
ǀ Dental	ɗ Dental/alveolar	p'	Bilabial
ǃ (Post)alveolar	ʄ Palatal	t'	Dental/alveolar
ǂ Palatoalveolar	ɠ Velar	k'	Velar
ǁ Alveolar lateral	ʛ Uvular	s'	Alveolar fricative

VOWELS

Where symbols appear in pairs, the one to the right represents a rounded vowel.

OTHER SYMBOLS

ʍ Voiceless labial-velar fricative

w Voiced labial-velar approximant

ɥ Voiced labial-palatal approximant

ʜ Voiceless epiglottal fricative

ʢ Voiced epiglottal fricative

ʡ Epiglottal plosive

ɕ ʑ Alveolo-palatal fricatives

ɺ Alveolar lateral flap

ɧ Simultaneous ʃ and x

Affricates and double articulations can be represented by two symbols joined by a tie bar if necessary.   k͡p t͡s

SUPRASEGMENTALS

ˈ Primary stress

ˌ Secondary stress   ˌfoʊnəˈtɪʃən

ː Long   eː

ˑ Half-long   eˑ

˘ Extra-short   ĕ

| Minor (foot) group

‖ Major (intonation) group

. Syllable break   ɹi.ækt

‿ Linking (absence of a break)

DIACRITICS   Diacritics may be placed above a symbol with a descender, e.g. ŋ̊

̥ Voiceless	n̥ d̥	̤ Breathy voiced	b̤ a̤	̪ Dental	t̪ d̪
̬ Voiced	s̬ t̬	̰ Creaky voiced	b̰ a̰	̺ Apical	t̺ d̺
ʰ Aspirated	tʰ dʰ	̼ Linguolabial	t̼ d̼	̻ Laminal	t̻ d̻
̹ More rounded	ɔ̹	ʷ Labialized	tʷ dʷ	̃ Nasalized	ẽ
̜ Less rounded	ɔ̜	ʲ Palatalized	tʲ dʲ	ⁿ Nasal release	dⁿ
̟ Advanced	u̟	ˠ Velarized	tˠ dˠ	ˡ Lateral release	dˡ
̠ Retracted	e̠	ˤ Pharyngealized	tˤ dˤ	̚ No audible release	d̚
̈ Centralized	ë	̴ Velarized or pharyngealized	ɫ		
̽ Mid-centralized	e̽	̝ Raised	e̝	(ɹ̝ = voiced alveolar fricative)	
̩ Syllabic	n̩	̞ Lowered	e̞	(β̞ = voiced bilabial approximant)	
̯ Non-syllabic	e̯	̘ Advanced Tongue Root	e̘		
˞ Rhoticity	ɚ a˞	̙ Retracted Tongue Root	e̙		

TONES AND WORD ACCENTS

LEVEL		CONTOUR	
e̋ or ˥ Extra high		ě or ◌̌ Rising	
é ˦ High		ê ◌̂ Falling	
ē ˧ Mid		é ˦˥ High rising	
è ˨ Low		è ˩˨ Low rising	
ȅ ˩ Extra low		ẽ ◌̃ Rising-falling	
↓ Downstep		↗ Global rise	
↑ Upstep		↘ Global fall	

Figure 2   The International Phonetic Alphabet
(revised to 1993, corrected 1996)

1

English Phonetics: Consonants (i)

1.1 Airstream and Articulation

Speech sounds are made by modifying an airstream. The airstream we will be concerned with in this book involves the passage of air from the lungs out through the **oral** and **nasal cavities** (see figure 1). There are many *points* at which that stream of air can be modified, and several *ways* in which it can be modified (i.e. constricted in some way). The first point at which the flow of air can be modified, as it passes from the lungs, is in the **larynx** (you can feel the front of this, the Adam's apple, protruding slightly at the front of your throat; see figure 1), in which are located the **vocal folds** (or vocal **cords**). The vocal folds may lie open, in which case the airstream passes through them unimpeded. Viewed from above, the vocal folds, when they lie open, look like this:

Open vocal folds

The vocal folds may be brought together so that they are closed, and no air may flow through them from the lungs:

1

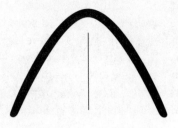

Closed vocal folds

One way in which the outgoing stream of air may be modified is by applying a certain level of constant muscular pressure sufficient to close the vocal folds along their length, but only just; the build-up of air pressure underneath this closure is sufficient, given the degree of muscular pressure, to force that closure open, but the air pressure then drops, and the muscular pressure causes the folds to close again. The sequence is then repeated, very rapidly, and results in what is called vocal fold vibration. You should be able to feel this vibration if you put your fingers to your larynx and produce the sound which is written as <z> in the word *hazy* (although you will probably also feel vibration elsewhere in your head). Sounds which are produced with this vocal fold vibration are said to be **voiced** sounds, whereas sounds produced without such vibration are said to be **voiceless**.

To transcribe speech sounds, phoneticians use the International Phonetic Alphabet (the IPA: see figure 2); the IPA symbol for the sound written <z> in *hazy* is [z]. You should be able to feel the presence of vibration in [z] if you put your fingers to your larynx and produce [z], then [s] (as in *miss*), then [z] again: [z] is voiced, whereas [s] is voiceless. This distinction will constitute the first of three descriptive parameters by means of which we will describe a given consonantal speech sound: we will say, for any given consonant, whether it is voiced or voiceless.

1.2 Place of Articulation

We will refer to the points at which the flow of air can be modified as places of articulation. We have just identified the vocal folds as a place of articulation; since the space between the vocal cords is referred to as the glottis, we will refer to sounds produced at this place of articulation as **glottal** sounds. There are many other places of articulation; we will identify a further seven.

Firstly, sounds in which the airflow is modified by forming a constriction between the lower lip and the upper lip are referred to as **bilabial** sounds. An example is the first sound in *pit*.

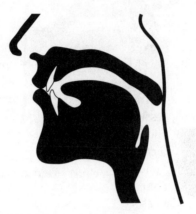

A bilabial sound: the first sound in *pit*

Secondly, sounds in which there is a constriction between the lower lip and the upper teeth are referred to as **labio-dental** sounds. An example is the first sound in *fit*.

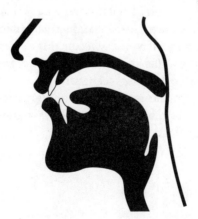

A labio-dental sound: the first sound in *fit*

Thirdly, sounds in which there is a constriction between the tip of the tongue and the upper teeth are referred to as **dental** sounds. An example is the first sound in *thin*.

A dental sound: the first sound in *thin*

For the remaining places of articulation, let us distinguish between the tip, the blade of the tongue, the front of the tongue and the back of the tongue (as in figure 1). Let us also distinguish various points along the upper part of the mouth. We will identify four different areas: the **alveolar ridge** (the hard, bony ridge behind the teeth; see figure 1), the **hard palate** (the hard, bony part of the roof of the mouth; see figure 1), the **palato-alveolar (or post-alveolar) region**[1] (the area in between the alveolar ridge and the hard palate), and the **velum** (the soft part at the back of the roof of the mouth, also known as the **soft palate**; see figure 1).

Sounds in which there is a constriction between the blade or tip of the tongue and the alveolar ridge are called **alveolar** sounds. An example is the first sound in *sin*.

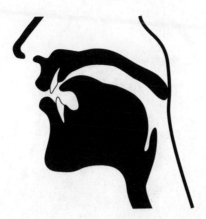

An alveolar sound: the first sound in *sin*

Sounds in which there is a constriction between the blade of the tongue and the palato-alveolar (or post-alveolar) region are called **palato-alveolar** sounds. An example is the first sound in *ship*.

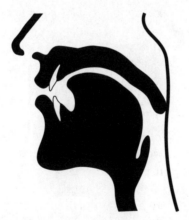

A palato-alveolar sound: the first sound in *ship*

Sounds in which there is a constriction between the front of the tongue and the hard palate are called **palatal** sounds. An example is the first sound in *yes* (although this may be less obvious to you; we will return to this sound below).

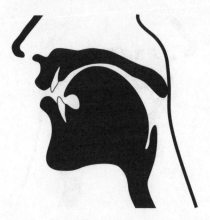

A palatal sound: the first sound in *yes*

Sounds in which there is a constriction between the back of the tongue and the velum are called **velar** sounds. An example is the first sound in *cool*.

A velar sound: the first sound in *cool*

1.3 Manner of Articulation: Stops, Fricatives and Approximants

We have now identified eight places of articulation: glottal, bilabial, labio-dental, dental, alveolar, palato-alveolar, palatal and velar. For any given sound we will say whether it is voiced or voiceless, and what its place of articulation is. But to distinguish between the full range of speech sounds, we will require a third descriptive parameter: **manner of articulation**. To identify the manner in which a sound is articulated, we will identify three different *degrees of constriction* (complete closure, close approximation and open approximation), and thus three different categories of consonant: stops, fricatives and approximants.

1.3.1   Stops

The articulators in question may form a stricture of **complete closure**; this is what happens when one produces the first sound in *pit*. Here the lower and upper lips completely block the flow of air from the lungs; that closure may then be released, as it is in *pit*, and may then produce a sudden outflow of air. Sounds which are produced with complete closure are referred to as **stops** (or **plosives**).

We may describe the first sound in *pit* as a voiceless bilabial stop (transcribed as [p]) and we will henceforth identify all consonants with three-term labels of this sort. The consonant in *abbey* is also a bilabial stop, but differs from that in *pit*: it is voiced. This consonant (transcribed as [b]) is a voiced bilabial stop.

The first sound in *tin* is a voiceless alveolar stop; it is transcribed as [t]. Its voiced counterpart is the consonant in *ado*. This sound, the voiced alveolar stop, is transcribed as [d].

The first sound in *cool* is a voiceless velar stop; it is transcribed as [k]. Its voiced counterpart, the voiced velar stop, is transcribed as [g]; an example is the consonant in *ago*.

We have now identified bilabial, alveolar and velar stops; stops may be made at many other places of articulation, but we will ignore those, as they are not relevant to the study of English. There is one further stop which we must mention, however, as it is very common in the speech of most speakers of English. This is the **glottal stop** (transcribed as [ʔ]). It is made by forming a constriction of complete closure between the vocal folds. This is the sound made instead of [t] in many Scottish and Cockney pronunciations of, for example, the word *butter*. We will see that it is present in the speech of almost every speaker of English, no matter what the accent.

There is no question of describing the glottal stop as voiced or voice-less, since it is articulated in the glottis itself.

1.3.2 Fricatives

Let us now distinguish between complete closure and another, less extreme, degree of constriction: **close approximation**. Sounds which are produced with this kind of constriction entail a bringing together of the two articulators to the point where the airflow is not quite fully blocked: enough of a gap remains for air to escape, but the articulators are so close together that friction is created as the air escapes. Sounds of this sort are referred to as **fricatives**.

The first sound in *fin* is created by bringing the lower lip close to the upper teeth in a constriction of close approximation. This sound is a voiceless labio-dental fricative (transcribed as [f]). Its voiced counterpart (the voiced labio-dental fricative, transcribed as [v]) is the consonant in *Eva*.

The first sound in *thin* is created by bringing the tip of the tongue into a constriction of close approximation with the upper teeth. This sound is a voiceless dental fricative, transcribed as [θ]. Its voiced counterpart, the voiced dental fricative (transcribed as [ð]) is, for some speakers, the first sound in the word *that*.[2]

The first sound in *sin* is created by bringing the tip or blade of the tongue into a constriction of close approximation with the alveolar ridge. This sound, transcribed as [s], is a voiceless alveolar fricative. Its voiced counterpart, the voiced alveolar fricative (trans-cribed as [z]) is the consonant in *zoo*.

The first sound in *ship* is created by bringing the blade of the tongue into a constriction of close approximation with the palato-alveolar region. This sound, transcribed as [ʃ], is a voiceless palato-alveolar fricative. Its voiced counterpart, transcribed as [ʒ], is the second con-sonant in *seizure*.

Fricatives may be articulated at any point of articulation, but many of those sounds are irrelevant to the study of English. However, we will mention three.

One is the voiceless velar fricative [x], found in the speech of many Scots, in words such as *loch*. Another is the voiceless fricative [ʍ], again found in the speech of many Scots, as in words like *whale* (as opposed to *wail*) and *which* (as opposed to *witch*; its place of articulation is labial-velar (explained in 1.3.3).

A third is the glottal fricative [h], as in the first sound in *hit*. This sound is produced by bringing the vocal cords into a constriction of close approximation, so that friction is produced. As the vocal cords are not vibrating, we will take it that this is a voiceless sound.

1.3.3 Approximants

The least radical degree of constriction occurs when the articulators come fairly close together, but not sufficiently close together to create friction. This kind of stricture is called **open approximation**. Consonants produced in this way are called **approximants**.

The first sound in *yes* is an approximant. It is produced by bringing the front of the tongue close to the hard palate. Although the sides of the tongue are in a constriction of complete closure with the upper gums, the air escapes along a central groove in which the front of the tongue is not close enough to the hard palate to create friction. This sound, transcribed as [j], is a voiced palatal approximant. Approximants are normally voiced, so we will not discuss any voiceless counterparts for these sounds.

The first sound in many English speakers' pronunciation of *rip, rope, rat*, etc. is an approximant. It is produced by bringing the blade of the tongue into a constriction of open approximation with the alveolar ridge. This approximant, transcribed as [ɹ], is referred to as an alveolar approximant. As with [j], the sides of the tongue form a constriction of complete closure with the gums at the sides of the mouth, but the air escapes along a central groove without creating friction. For most speakers (and in varying degrees, depending on the accent), the tongue body is somewhat retracted when [ɹ] is uttered; it is therefore often referred to as a *post*-alveolar approximant, but 'alveolar approximant' will suffice for our purposes.[3]

We will be looking at more English approximants in chapter 2. For the moment, let us identify one further such sound, the sound at the beginning of *wet*. In producing this sound, the lips form a constriction of open approximation: there is no friction produced. But its articulation is more complicated than that of [j], the palatal approximant, since it also involves another articulation, between the back of the tongue and the velum (i.e. a velar articulation). We will therefore refer to it as a voiced *labial-velar* approximant; it is transcribed as [w].

Notes

1. Many phonologists and phoneticians use the term 'palato-alveolar', but the chart of symbols used by the International Phonetics Association uses the term 'post-alveolar'. It will suffice for our purposes if the student takes the two terms to be interchangeable. There are no rigid physiological divisions between the alveolar ridge and the hard palate; the transition from one to the other is a continuum. And the range of articulations which can be made in between the two is relatively varied, leading some phoneticians to distinguish alveo-palatal from palato-alveolar articulations. We will simplify by ignoring these details.
2. Many speakers of English do not have a voiced dental fricative; rather, the sound lacks friction: it is a voiced dental approximant.
3. The articulation of an [ɹ] kind of articulation in some American and West Country accents is also referred to by some as *retroflex* approximant. The term 'retroflex' means that blade and tip of the tongue are curled upwards and backwards to some extent, so that the underside of a part of the tongue forms the relevant articulation. Somewhat inaccurately, we will use [ɹ] for these sounds.

Exercises

1. Give the appropriate three-term description for each of the following sounds (e.g. [k]: voiceless velar stop):

   [f] [b] [θ] [ʃ] [t] [j]

2. Give the appropriate phonetic symbol for each of the following sounds:

   (a) a voiced palato-alveolar fricative
   (b) a voiced alveolar stop
   (c) a voiced velar stop

(d)   a voiced dental fricative
(e)   a voiced labio-dental fricative

3   What phonetic property distinguishes each of the following pairs of sounds (e.g. [p] and [b]: voicing; [s] and [ʃ]: place of articulation; [t] and [s]: manner of articulation)?

(a)   [k] and [g]   (b)   [b] and [d]   (c)   [d] and [z]
(d)   [z] and [ʒ]   (e)   [ʃ] and [ʒ]   (f)   [d] and [g]

4   Which of the following English words begin with a fricative?

*ship   psychology   veer   round   plot   philosophy   think
late   xylophone*

5   Which of the following English words end with a fricative?

*stack   whale   swim   epitaph   half   halve   hash   haze   phase
use   path   cuts   pleads*

6   Which of the following English words begin with a stop?

*philanderer   plasterer   parsimonious   ptarmigan   psyche
charismatic   cereal   carping   kinky   ghoulish   gruelling
guardian   thick   tickle   bin   dreary*

7   Describe the position and action of the articulators during the production of the following sounds (e.g. [d]: the blade of the tongue forms a constriction of complete closure with the alveolar ridge; the vocal cords are vibrating):

[b]   [k]   [θ]   [v]

2

English Phonetics: Consonants (ii)

2.1 Central vs Lateral

In discussing the alveolar approximant [ɹ], we said that the air escapes along a central groove (of the tongue, in this case; the same kind of groove can be formed by the lips). This is true for all of the fricatives and approximants described in chapter 1: they are all *central* fricatives and approximants. However, it is possible to produce fricatives and approximants in which this is not the case. For instance, in the first sound in *lift*, the centre of the blade of the tongue forms a stricture of complete closure with part of the alveolar ridge, but the articulation which 'counts' is that between the *sides* of the tongue and the alveolar ridge. Since the sides of the tongue form a constriction of open articulation with the alveolar ridge, and no friction is created, we refer to this sound (transcribed as [l]) as a voiced alveolar lateral approximant. Since English fricatives and approximants are typically central, we will use the term 'lateral' for laterals, and omit the term 'central' in describing central fricatives and approximants in English speech. The sounds [l] and [ɹ] are, clearly, quite similar: both are approximants, both are voiced, both are alveolar. The principal difference is that the former is lateral and the latter central.[1]

2.2 Taps and Trills

We have said that, for a great many speakers of English, the sound at the beginning of words such as *rat, rope, reap*, etc. is a post-alveolar approximant: [ɹ]. The same is true of the sound which occurs after stops in words such as *prude, true, creep*, etc. However, some speakers utter, not an approximant, but a sound which is very like a voiced alveolar stop of very short duration. Many Scots utter this sound, rather than [ɹ], after stops, as in the words just cited. During the articulation of this sound, the blade of the tongue comes into a momentary constriction of complete closure with the alveolar ridge. This sound, transcribed as [ɾ], is referred to as a voiced alveolar **tap** (or flap). This is also the sound that many American speakers have instead of [t] or [d] in words such as *Betty, witty, rider, heady*, etc.

Speakers of certain accents of English may utter neither an [ɾ] nor an [ɹ] in words such as *rat, rope, reap* and *prude, true, creep*, but a sound referred to as a voiced alveolar **trill**. Trills are produced by holding one articulator (e.g. the blade of the tongue) next to the other (e.g. the alveolar ridge) in a constriction of complete closure, but without the same muscular pressure as one finds in stops. The result is that air pressure builds up behind the closure and forces it open; the air pressure then reduces, and the muscular pressure again creates a constriction of complete closure. This sequence may be repeated in quick succession, producing, in the case of an alveolar trill, a series of taps of the tongue against the alveolar ridge. The alveolar trill is transcribed as [r], but is relatively rare. Scots are often said to produce this sound; however, most speakers of Scottish varieties of English typically produce, not an alveolar trill, but an alveolar tap.

2.3 Secondary Articulation

We have said that the lateral approximant [l] is alveolar. However, laterals may also be produced with an additional articulation, such as one formed between the back of the tongue and the velum, i.e. a velar articulation. When this happens, we may distinguish between the alveolar articulation as the **primary articulation** and the velar one as the **secondary articulation**. Where a secondary articulation is velar, this process is referred to as **velarization**: we say that the lateral is velarized. A velarized lateral approximant is transcribed using the velarization diacritic, thus: [ɫ]. This sound is often referred to as **'dark l'**.[2] Where a secondary articulation is palatal (formed between the front of the tongue and the hard palate), this process is referred to as **palatalization**; we say that the lateral is palatalized. A palatalized lateral is transcribed using the palatalization diacritic, thus: [lʲ]. The term **'clear l'** is often used to refer to [lʲ], or to [l] (neither palatalized nor 'dark'). In subsequent chapters, we will consider the status of 'dark l' and 'clear l' in different accents of English.

2.4 Affricates

We have, thus far, distinguished three classes of consonant according to degree of constriction: stops, fricatives and approximants. Consider the first sound in *chip*: it is like a stop in that there is complete closure between the blade of the tongue and the palato-alveolar region. However, it is like a fricative in that it clearly involves friction. That friction occurs during the *release phase* of the closure, which we referred to in 1.3.1. Sounds produced with a constriction of complete closure followed by a release phase in which friction occurs are called **affricates**. We might say that one of the main differences (place of articulation apart) between the first sound in *tip* and the first sound in *chip* is that, during the release phase of the [t] in *tip*, there is no friction of the sort one finds during the release phase of the first sound in *chip*. We might therefore think of affricates as stops with a slow, fricative, release phase. The affricate in *chip* is a voiceless palato-alveolar affricate, transcribed as [tʃ]. Its voiced counterpart is [dʒ], the first sound in *jury, joy*, etc.[3]

These two affricates occur in the speech of most speakers of English. In later chapters, we will examine some other affricates which occur in the speech of speakers of certain accents of English.

2.5 Aspiration

The first stop in *pit*, we said, is a voiceless bilabial stop. So too is the first stop in *spit*. But the bilabial stop in *pit* differs phonetically from the bilabial stop in *spit*: if you hold the palm of your hand up close to your mouth when uttering *pit*, you will feel a stronger puff of air on releasing the bilabial stop than you will when you utter *spit*. That 'stronger puff of air' phenomenon is called **aspiration**: we say that the bilabial stop in *pit* is an *aspirated* voiceless stop, whereas the stop in *spit* is *unaspirated*. Aspirated voiceless stops are transcribed with the aspiration diacritic ([ʰ]), so that the bilabial stop in *pit* is transcribed as [pʰ]. Unaspirated stops are transcribed without that diacritic, so that the bilabial stop in *spit* is transcribed as [p].

2.6 Nasal Stops

We have been making an assumption in our discussion thus far, concerning the position of the velum in the production of the speech sounds we have described. We have assumed that, in all of these sounds, the air from the lungs is escaping only through the mouth (the oral cavity). This is true if the velum is in the *raised* position, such that it prevents the flow of air out through the nasal cavity (see figure 1). In all of the sounds discussed thus far, the velum is indeed raised: we describe all such sounds as **oral** sounds. But the velum may be lowered, to allow escape of air through the nasal cavity (see figure 1). Sounds produced with the velum lowered, and with air escaping through the nasal cavity alone, are referred to as **nasal stops**.[4] These may occur at most places of articulation; let us consider those which are relevant for the study of English.

While nasal stops may be either voiced or voiceless, they are typically voiced in most human languages; we will therefore ignore voiceless nasal stops and use the term 'nasal stop' to imply '*voiced* nasal stop'.

Bilabial nasal stops (transcribed [m]) entail, as one would expect, complete closure between the lips, voicing, and escape of the air through the nasal cavity. An example is the first consonant in *map*.

Labio-dental nasal stops (transcribed [ɱ]) entail complete closure between the lower lip and the upper teeth, voicing, and escape of the air through the nasal cavity. An example is the second consonant in *pamphlet*. In English, they occur before labio-dental sounds, as in this case. The nasal stop articulation in cases such as these reflects a process of **assimilation**. Assimilation processes are processes in which one sound becomes similar to an adjacent sound. In this case, the nasal is assimilated to the following fricative, in the sense that it 'takes on' the place of articulation of the fricative. Such processes involve a principle of **ease of articulation**. In this case, if the nasal in *pamphlet* is articulated at the same place as the following fricative, this saves the speaker the articulatory effort of moving from a bilabial to a labio-dental articulation. We will return to such processes in chapter 6.

Dental nasal stops (transcribed [n̪]) entail complete closure between the tip of the tongue and the upper teeth, voicing, and escape of the air through the nasal cavity. An example is the second consonant in *tenth*. As in this case, they occur before other dental sounds, and this too is a matter of assimilation involving place of articulation.

Alveolar nasal stops (transcribed as [n]) entail complete closure between the blade of the tongue and the alveolar ridge, voicing, and escape of the air through the nasal cavity. An example is the first sound in *not*.

Velar nasal stops (transcribed as [ŋ]) entail complete closure between the back of the tongue and the velum, voicing and escape of air through the nasal cavity. An example is the last sound in *sing* or the nasal stop as it is often articulated (especially in faster or more casual speech styles) in the word *incredible*. Once again, the latter case involves assimilation.

Notes

1   The central approximant [ɹ] also differs from [l] in having tongue body retraction and lip rounding. We will see shortly that alveolar laterals may be produced with retraction too.

2 The term 'dark l' can also be used to refer to lateral approximants in which the body/back of the tongue is retracted and/or lowered. Accents of English vary with respect to the exact articulatory nature of their 'dark l's: some are velarized, while others have no velar articulation, but have, instead, retraction and/or lowering of the back/body of the tongue. Such retraction can lead to loss of alveolar contact, and thus to [l]-vocalization, in which the articulation becomes vowel-like.

3 Some authors transcribe [ʧ] as [č] and [ʤ] as [ǰ]. We should, if we were to stick strictly to the conventions of the International Phonetics Association, transcribe both affricates with a 'tie bar' above the two symbols; we depart here from the conventions of the IPA chart, which does not contain an 'affricate' category.

4 The term 'nasalized', as opposed to 'nasal', is used to describe sounds in which air escapes through *both* cavities, the oral *and* the nasal. The term 'nasal' is used to describe sounds in which the air escapes through the nasal cavity alone.

Exercises

1 For each of the following English words, identify (a) any oral stops, (b) any fricatives, (c) any approximants, (d) any affricates and (e) any nasals. For each sound that you identify, say whether it is voiced or voiceless and what its place of articulation is (e.g. the word *stop*: voiceless alveolar stop [t] and voiceless bilabial stop [p]; voiceless alveolar fricative [s]; no approximants, affricates or nasals):

bring licking fever thinking assure measure heated years worm jungle

2 Which of the following words begins with an affricate, and which (if any) with a stop, in your speech? Transcribe any variation in how you pronounce any of these words, depending on how 'carefully' you pronounce them.

tune chip dune June

English Phonetics: Consonants (ii)

Many speakers of English typically utter words like *tune* and *dune* with an affricate at the beginning of the word. This means that *dune* and *June* are typically indistinguishable. None the less, when asked in a phonetics class whether they utter words such as *dune* with an affricate, such speakers often deny that they do. These speakers typically have a more careful pronunciation of words such as *tune* and *dune*, in which there *is* a [j].

Notice, however, that there is no such more careful pronunciation of words like *chip* and *June*: one never hears these pronounced with [tj] and [dj]. In order to explain the difference between *dune* and *June*, we need to say that the speaker in some sense intends to utter [dj] in *dune*, but that ease of articulation results in a palato-alveolar affricated release of the stop closure, rather than a transition from an alveolar closure to a stricture of open approximation between the front of the tongue and the hard palate. In the case of *June* and *chip*, the intended articulation is a palato-alveolar affricate.

If you are a speaker of General American, you may well never utter a [j] in words like *tune* and *dune*, in which case you will utter a stop followed by a vowel. However, you may well also have been told at school that the 'correct' pronunciation of such words has a [j] after the stop. Your speech may well vary with respect to the presence or absence of the [j]. If your speech does vary in this way, how do you pronounce *noon*?

3 Give a phonetic transcription of each of the following words, using a 'V' for the vowels:

*lull   pear   reap   throws   think   misjudges   churches
incorrect   input*

You may well have noticed that the nasal stop in *think* is velar, rather than alveolar. It requires considerable conscious effort to utter that nasal stop as alveolar, and when one does so, the resulting pronunciation sounds quite unnatural. This appears to be the result of a process of anticipatory assimilation: the tongue adopts the articulatory position for the velar stop [k] during the pronunciation of the nasal.

18

But what about the nasal-plus-velar stop sequence in *incorrect*? Many speakers of English find it easier to utter an alveolar, rather than a velar, nasal there, despite the fact that cases like *incorrect* also contain a sequence of a nasal stop followed by a velar stop. Do you have any hunches as to why the two cases should be different?

3

English Phonetics: Vowels (i)

3.1 The Primary Cardinal Vowels

Let us begin by assuming that all vowels are voiced and are articulated with a constriction of open approximation. We will also assume, for the moment, that all vowels are *oral* sounds (i.e. that the velum is raised during their production). The range of positions which the tongue can occupy within the oral cavity while remaining in a constriction of open approximation is quite large. Let us call the entire available space for such articulations the **vowel space**. We will require a means of plotting the point at which a given vowel is articulated in the vowel space. In order to do this, we will appeal to an idealized chart of that space, as follows (this chart is repeated in the IPA chart in figure 2):

(1)   The vowel space and the primary cardinal vowels

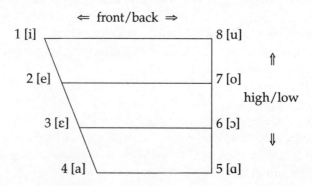

English Phonetics: Vowels (i)

In this diagram, we represent the vowel space along two dimensions. The first is the **high/low** dimension (also referred to as the close/open dimension), depicting the height of the body of the tongue during the articulation of a vowel (i.e. depicting *vowel height*). This is represented as the vertical axis in the diagram. The second is the **back/front** dimension, depicting the extent to which the body of the tongue lies towards the front of the vowel space. This is represented as the horizontal axis in the diagram. We may identify three arbitrary points along this dimension: **front, central** and **back**. In using these two dimensions, we can say, for any given vowel, how high in the vowel space it is articulated, and whether it is a front, central or back vowel. To these two descriptive parameters, we will add a third, which refers to lip position: we will say, for a given vowel, whether, during its articulation, the lips are rounded or not. We will refer to the former sort of vowel as a **rounded** vowel and the latter as an **unrounded** vowel.

It is convenient to identify several points along the perimeter of the vowel space. Once we have done this, we can plot the location of any given vowel in relation to those points. Vowels articulated at those points are called **the cardinal vowels**. We will now identify eight of them.

Let us begin with the vowel which is produced when the lips are unrounded and the tongue is located as high as possible and as front as possible, without causing friction, in the vowel space. This is **cardinal vowel no. 1**, depicted at the top left-hand corner of the diagram in (1) above. That vowel is transcribed as [i]. Using our three descriptive parameters, we will refer to this as a high front unrounded vowel. We will not seek to exemplify cardinal vowels with words from English, or any other language, since, typically, speakers do not utter vowel sounds which are quite as peripheral in the vowel space as the cardinal vowels. The vowel in many English speakers' pronunciation of the word *peep*, for instance, is quite close to cardinal vowel no. 1: it too is a **high front rounded vowel**, but it is not quite as *peripheral* as cardinal vowel no. 1: it is typically slightly less high and slightly less front in its articulation.

Let us now identify the cardinal vowel which lies at the 'opposite end' of the vowel space: the vowel which is produced when the lips are unrounded and the body of the tongue is as low as possible

21

and as far back as possible, without causing friction. This is **cardinal vowel no. 5**. Its location is depicted at the bottom right-hand corner of the diagram in (1) above. Transcribed as [ɑ], it is a **low back unrounded vowel**.

We have now identified two 'anchor' points in the vowel space; we may now proceed to identify further cardinal vowels in relation to these. If the lips remain unrounded and the body of the tongue remains as low as possible in the vowel space (as for cardinal vowel no. 5), but the tongue is moved as far to the front of that space as is possible without causing friction, then **cardinal vowel no. 4** is produced. It is transcribed as [a].

We have now identified two vowel heights: high and low. You should be able to feel this difference in tongue height if you utter cardinal vowel no. 1 followed by cardinal vowel no. 4: the jaw opens considerably and the body of the tongue lowers considerably as one moves from the former to the latter. There is a continuum of vowel heights between these two heights; we will identify two arbitrary points along this continuum: **high-mid** and **low-mid**. If the lips remain unrounded and the body of the tongue remains as far front as is possible, but the tongue height is lowered somewhat from the cardinal vowel no. 1 position, one arrives at the front, **high-mid unrounded vowel** known as **cardinal vowel no. 2**. This is transcribed as [e].

In retaining the same lip position and the same degree of frontness, one may lower the body of the tongue further still to the low-mid position, and arrive at the **front low-mid unrounded vowel** known as **cardinal vowel no. 3**. This is transcribed as [ɛ].

If you articulate cardinal vowel no. 1, then cardinal vowels nos. 2, 3 and 4, you should feel the body of the tongue lowering progressively. These are all front unrounded vowels: the difference between them lies in the height of the tongue.

Let us now consider the back cardinal vowels. If the body of the tongue is as high as possible and as far back as possible without causing friction, and the lips are, this time, rounded, then **cardinal vowel no. 8** is produced. This **high back rounded vowel** is transcribed as [u].

If the lips remain rounded and the tongue remains as far back as possible, but the tongue height is lowered to the high-mid position,

cardinal vowel no. 7 is produced. This **high-mid back rounded vowel** is transcribed as [o].

In retaining the same degree of backness and the same lip position, one may lower the height of the tongue still further, to the low-mid position, and thus produce the **low-mid back rounded vowel** known as **cardinal vowel no. 6**. This is transcribed as [ɔ].

You should be able to feel the tongue lowering progressively as you make the transition from cardinal vowel no. 8, through cardinal vowel no. 7, to cardinal vowel no. 6; the tongue goes through the same lowering process as it does for the transition from cardinal vowel no. 1, through no. 2, to no. 3.

We have now identified the eight primary cardinal vowels. With these reference points established, we may describe the articulation of specific English vowels in relation to them. Let us begin by looking at those referred to as the English short vowels.

3.2 RP and GA Short Vowels

There is considerable variation in the vowel sounds uttered by speakers of different accents of English, and we will be considering that variation in later chapters. For the moment, we will begin with two particular accents; we will later describe others. We will, somewhat arbitrarily, begin with the accents known as **Received Pronunciation (RP)** and **General American (GA)**. RP is the accent often referred to as the 'prestige' accent in British society and associated with the speech of the graduates of the English public schools. It is thus defined largely in terms of the social class of its speakers. We do not select it as one of our starting points for that reason; rather, we select it as it tends to be the accent which foreign learners of British English are taught, and has thus been widely described. GA tends to be defined in terms of the geographical location, rather than the social class, of its speakers. The term 'GA' is an idealization over a group of accents whose speakers inhabit a vast proportion of the United States: it excludes Eastern accents such as the New York City accent, and Southern accents (such as that spoken in Texas).

It has often been pointed out that terms such as 'RP' and 'GA' entail a great deal of idealization, in that they are used to cover a variety of somewhat different, if converging, accents. We accept this as inevitable: it will be true of any term we use to describe an accent (e.g. 'New York City', 'Cockney', 'Scouse', 'Geordie', South African', etc.) and indeed it is true of the term 'accent' itself. But we need some way of expressing valid generalizations about the speech sounds which members of different speech communities utter. For instance, it is generally true that, while RP speakers pronounce *put* and *putt* differently, many speakers with accents found in the North of England do not. To refuse to speak of different accents would be to throw the baby out with the bathwater, and to deny ourselves the opportunity of expressing statements which are informative, if subject to certain caveats.

We have said nothing, as yet, about the length of vowels. For speakers of RP and GA, the vowels in *peep* and *pip* differ in several respects, one of which is vowel length. If you are an RP or a GA speaker, and you utter the two words, you will probably agree that the vowel in the former is longer than that in the latter. We will, accordingly, refer to the former as a long vowel and the latter as a short vowel. Vowel length is a relative matter: when we say that the vowel in *pip* is a short vowel, we are not referring to its duration in milliseconds; rather, we are saying that it is short in relation to other vowels, such as that in *peep*. The vowel in *pip* is typically articulated with the body of the tongue fairly front and fairly high, and with the lips unrounded. We will transcribe that vowel as [ɪ]. While it is a high front unrounded vowel, it is less high and less front than the vowel in *peep*. Its location is depicted in (2) below.

Now consider the vowel in RP and GA speakers' pronunciation of the vowel in the word *put*. This is, for many speakers, a high back rounded vowel, articulated in the region near to cardinal vowel no. 8. It is similar to the vowel in *school*, but less high and less back. It is also shorter than that in *school*. We will transcribe this short vowel as [ʊ]; its location is depicted in (2) below.

For RP and GA speakers, there is a distinction between the vowel in *put* and that in *putt*. Both are short vowels, but they differ in several respects. Firstly, the latter vowel is unrounded. Secondly, the vowel in *putt* is articulated with a fairly low tongue height: typically, it is just below the low-mid position. Thirdly, the vowel in *putt* is located at around the half-way point on the front/back axis. We will refer to vowels located in this region as **central** vowels. We will transcribe this vowel as [ʌ]; its location is depicted in (2) below.

In both RP and GA, the vowels in *aunt* and *ant* differ Both vowels are unrounded, but the vowel in *ant* is shorter than that in *aunt*, and the vowel in *ant* is a low front vowel, whereas that in *aunt* is a low back vowel. The low front unrounded vowel in *ant* is articulated higher and less front than cardinal vowel no. 4. We will transcribe this as [æ]; its location is depicted in (2) below (although the GA vowel is higher than the RP vowel, and sounds rather [ɛ]-like to British speakers).

The short vowel in RP and GA speakers' pronunciation of the word *bet* is a front unrounded vowel, whose height is somewhere between cardinal vowels nos. 2 and 3. For most RP and GA speakers, it is closer to cardinal vowel no. 3 than to cardinal vowel no. 2 in height; it is also somewhat more centralized than cardinal vowel no. 3. For convenience' sake, we will transcribe it as [ɛ]; its location is depicted in (2) below.

The short vowel in the RP speaker's pronunciation of the word *pot* is a back, rounded vowel which is articulated with a tongue height somewhere between low and low-mid (i.e. between cardinal vowels nos. 5 and 6). It is transcribed as [ɒ]; its location is given in (2) below. This vowel is absent from the GA system: GA speakers have the vowel [ɑ] in words such as *pot*. [ɑ] is a short back rounded low vowel.

(2)   RP and GA short vowels

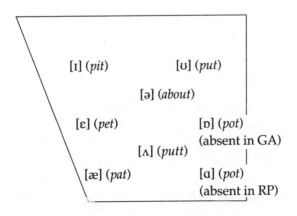

There is one further vowel sound, indicated above, which we must consider at this stage. It is the first vowel sound which occurs in most speakers' pronunciation of the word *about*. This vowel is referred to as **schwa**; it is produced without lip rounding, and with the body of the tongue lying in the most central part of the vowel space, between high-mid and low-mid, and between back and front. Schwa is transcribed as [ə]. This vowel is typically even shorter than the short vowels we have just described, and it differs from those in that it may never occur in a stressed syllable (in *about*, it occurs in the unstressed first syllable; in *elephant*, it occurs in the unstressed second syllable; in *Belinda*, it occurs in the unstressed initial and final syllables). This vowel occurs in the speech of almost every speaker of English; in later chapters, we will consider its relation to English stressed vowels in more detail.

Exercises

1 Describe the position of the body of the tongue and the lips in the production of the following vowels:

[i] (cardinal vowel no. 1)
[u] (cardinal vowel no. 8)
[ɑ] (cardinal vowel no. 5)

2 Give an appropriate vowel symbol for the vowel in each of the following words, as you would utter them. Say (a) whether the vowel is rounded or not, (b) how back or front it is, and (c) how low or high it is (do this in relation to the cardinal vowels):

pit apt stock bet put putt

Note. If you are discussing these exercises in a tutorial group, you may well already have begun to notice differences in the speech of the members of the group, depending on the accents they speak. Clearly, there is little point, if one has, say, a West Yorkshire or a New York City accent, in transcribing these words *as if* one were an RP or a GA speaker. What you should do is to try to work out (preferably with the help of a tutor) what the quality of each vowel is, and to adopt an appropriate phonetic symbol for that vowel, which you can then use consistently in your transcriptions. In due course, we will be examining accent variation in more detail.

3 Give a phonetic transcription, with as much phonetic detail as possible, for each of the following words; do this by uttering them, listening to what you say, and then transcribing what you hear:

encourage   unbalanced   suspicious   throb   elephant

4
English Phonetics: Vowels (ii)

4.1 RP and GA Long Vowels

We noted that the RP/GA vowel in *put* ([ʊ]) is shorter than that in *school*; we also said that it is less back and less high than that in *school*. We will transcribe the vowel in *school* as [u:], where the ' : ' diacritic denotes vowel length. This is a high back rounded vowel, articulated closer to cardinal vowel 8 than [ʊ].

The RP/GA short vowel [ɪ], as in *fit*, which we described in chapter 3, is a fairly high, fairly front, unrounded vowel. It differs from the RP/GA vowel in *feet*, which is longer, more front and higher. We will transcribe this as [i:]; it is a high front unrounded vowel which is closer to cardinal vowel 1 than [ɪ].

It is worth noting that in RP and GA, when words such as *to* and *(s)he* are uttered in isolation, they contain, respectively, the vowels [u:] and [i:], so that *to* is pronounced in the same way as *two* and *too*. But 'function' words like *to* and *(s)he* (which are not nouns, adjectives or verbs) are often uttered without stress, in which case they may be uttered with a schwa ([ə]), or in a shortened form, as in *to eat* (pronounced either as [təi:t] or as [tui:t]) and *she wore* (pronounced either [ʃəwɔ:] or [ʃiwɔ:]). The shortened form of [i:] is also found in various suffixes, as in the suffix in *witty*: [wɪti] and in the suffix in *quickly*: [kʰwɪkli]. It occurs too in the unstressed syllable of words such as *pretty*: [pʰɹɪti].[1]

The RP vowel in *port* and *caught* is longer than that in *pot* and *cot*; it is a low-mid back rounded vowel, articulated closer to cardinal vowel 6 than is the [ɒ] in RP *pot* and *cot*. We will transcribe it as [ɔ:]. This is also the vowel which GA speakers utter in words like *caught* (although the GA vowel is somewhat shorter than the RP vowel). Thus, although both GA and RP speakers distinguish between pairs such as *cot* and *caught*, GA has [ɑ] in *cot* whereas RP speakers have [ɒ]. In GA, words such as *horse* and *port*, with an [ɹ] after the vowel, are typically uttered as [hɔɹs] and [pʰɔɹt] (see below on /oʊ/ in RP and GA).

The RP and GA short vowel [æ], as in *ant*, is, as we have seen, a fairly low, rather front, unrounded vowel. It differs from that in *aunt*, which is a low back unrounded vowel, articulated in the region of cardinal vowel 5. The RP/GA vowel in *aunt* is also longer than the RP/GA vowel in *ant*. We will transcribe it as [ɑ:]. Thus, whereas RP has a three-way distinction between [ɒ], [ɑ:] and [ɔ:], GA has only a two-way distinction between [ɑ] and [ɔ:]. We will return to this difference between the accents below.

RP and GA speakers utter a long vowel in words like *bird*, *heard*, *dearth*, although GA speakers utter an [ɹ] in words such as these, while RP speakers do not. The articulation for this vowel is pretty much the same as that for schwa: it is central on both the high/low and front/back dimensions, and is unrounded. Unlike schwa, it appears in stressed syllables. We will transcribe it as [ɜ:].

We may depict the approximate areas of articulation of these vowels in the vowel space as follows:

(1) RP and GA long vowels

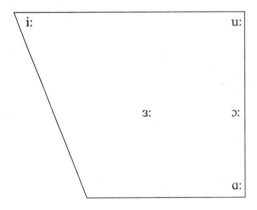

carted   concluded   divine   divinity   serene   serenity

Note (i). It can be rather a difficult task, at first, to listen consciously and attentively to the phonetic details of one's own speech while at the same time attempting to speak naturally, as if one were *not* listening; it involves playing a kind of psychological trick on oneself. However, it is possible, with a little practice, to get the hang of it.

Note (ii). Some students will have an [ɹ] (or an [r]) in *carted*, while others will not; transcribe it if you utter it, but do not transcribe it if you do not. We will return to variation with respect to [ɹ] in due course. See too the note under exercise 2, chapter 3.

5

The Phonemic Principle

5.1   Introduction: Linguistic Knowledge

We have been dealing, thus far, with phonetics, that is (as we
have defined it), with the study of human speech sounds (although
we have dealt exclusively with *English* phonetics, and in particular,
exclusively *articulatory* phonetics, ignoring important facts about the
acoustic properties of the speech sounds we have been discussing).
We will, henceforth, be dealing with *phonology*, as well as phonetics. Phonology, we will claim, is to do with something more than
properties of human speech sounds *per se*. Phonology is the study
of certain sorts of mental organization. In particular, it is the study
of certain types of mental category, mentally stored representations,
and generalizations concerning those categories and representations.
On this view, phonology is *not* the study of human speech sounds
per se, although phonetics and phonology are inextricably inter-
twined. The point of this chapter is to demonstrate what the difference between the two is, and to begin to introduce the reader to the
phonology of English. Let us begin by considering some general questions concerning what it is to know a language.

Let us assume that when we say that someone knows a language,
in the sense of being a native speaker of that language, he or she is
in a certain mental state, or possesses a certain sort of linguistic knowledge. Knowledge of a native language is, apparently, largely unconscious knowledge. It appears to contain semantic knowledge (to do
with the meanings of words, phrases and sentences) and syntactic

knowledge (to do with the syntactic categories of words, with the structure of phrases and sentences and with the syntactic relations between words, phrases and clauses). We know that this is so, since speakers are able to make syntactic and semantic judgements, based on that knowledge. For instance, a native speaker of English can judge that *Who did you see Graham with?* is an English sentence, and that *Who did you see Graham and?* is not. The speaker knows, again intuitively, that the difference between the two amounts to more than the difference between the mere presence of the word *and* as opposed to the presence of the word *with*. He or she also knows intuitively (not necessarily fully consciously) in what sense *He told the man who he knew* is ambiguous, and in what sense the two interpretations of that sequence of words differs in structure and meaning from *He told the man how he knew*, over and above the superficial fact that one sequence contains *who* and the other *how*. That knowledge is clearly unconscious knowledge, since we require no instruction to be able to make such judgements, and we can make them in the absence of any conscious knowledge whatsoever of the syntax and semantics of English (one could make such judgements even if one had not the faintest idea of what a noun or a verb might be, or what the syntactic categories of *with, and, who* and *how* might be).

We will take the view in this book that a speaker's (largely) unconscious knowledge of his or her native language(s) must also contain phonological knowledge. One of the reasons many linguists take this view is that speakers can make judgements which, it is claimed, are in some sense parallel to those made with respect to syntactic states of affairs. For instance, a native speaker of English can tell how many syllables there are in a word without having the faintest idea, consciously, as to what a syllable is. This shows that the native speaker has the ability to recognize syllables, even if the recognition of syllables lies below the level of consciousness. In a similar fashion, it is claimed, a native speaker of English can tell that the sequence of segments [blʌg], considered as an utterance of a word, is an English sequence, whereas the sequence of segments [tʰlʌg] is not, despite the fact that she or he may well never have heard either sequence in her or his life. Let us postulate that, in making such judgements, the native speaker of English gains access to a kind of unconscious knowledge which constitutes 'the phonology of English'.

Our task, in this book, will be to begin to consider, in an elementary way, what form that knowledge takes. The discipline of phonology, under this view, differs from that of phonetics, since it is the study, not of speech sounds *per se*, but of mental abilities and largely unconscious mental states. Clearly, the phonologist must pay close attention to speech sounds and their properties; they will constitute much of the evidence the phonologist brings to bear on his or her hypotheses about speakers' unconscious phonological knowledge, but they do not constitute his or her object of inquiry as such.

5.2 Contrast vs Predictability: The Phoneme

Let us begin by considering voiceless unaspirated and voiceless aspirated stops in English and Korean. Speakers of most accents of English habitually utter both aspirated and unaspirated voiceless stops. The following English data exhibit both of these.[1]

(1)   Aspirated and unaspirated voiceless stops in English

(a)	['pʰuːɫ]	'pool'	(b)	[ə'pʰɪə]	'appear'
(c)	['spɜːt]	'spurt'	(d)	[də'spaɪt]	'despite'
(e)	['tʰɒp]	'top'	(f)	[ə'tʰæk]	'attack'
(g)	['stɒp]	'stop'	(h)	[də'stɹɔɪ]	'destroy'
(i)	['kʰɪlɪŋ]	'killing'	(j)	[ə'kʰɹuː]	'accrue'
(k)	['skoʊɫd]	'scold'	(l)	[dɪ'skʌvə]	'discover'

The diacritic which precedes certain symbols in these data (the one which precedes the 'p' symbol in ['pʰuːɫ]) indicates the beginning of a stressed syllable. We will assume that it is evident to the reader which syllable in the above words is the stressed syllable (e.g. the first syllable in *killing* and the second syllable in *accrue*).

From these data, it appears that voiceless stops are aspirated when they are at the beginning of a stressed syllable, as in *pit* and *appear*, but unaspirated when preceded by a voiceless alveolar fricative, as in *spurt*. That is, in these data, wherever the unaspirated voiceless stops appear, the aspirated ones do not, and vice versa. Compare the English data with the following data from Korean:

37

(2)   Aspirated and unaspirated voiceless stops in Korean

(a)	[pʰul]	'grass'	(b)	[pul]	'fire'
(c)	[tʰal]	'mask'	(d)	[tal]	'moon'
(e)	[kʰɛda]	'dig'	(f)	[kɛda]	'fold'

In these Korean data, aspirated and unaspirated voiceless stops may occur in the same place (at the beginning of a word). The range of places within a word which a given sound may occur in is called its **distribution**. In the English data we have looked at, the distribution of unaspirated and aspirated stops is *mutually exclusive*: where you get one kind of stop, you never get the other. This is called **complementary distribution**.

Furthermore, if we take, say, the stops [t] and [tʰ] in the English data, it is clear that they are **phonetically similar**: both are stops, both are voiceless, both are alveolar. And yet, for most speakers of English, the alveolar stops in, say, *still* and *till* sound the same, despite the fact that the former is unaspirated and the latter aspirated. For the English speaker, these two phonetically distinct sounds 'count as the same thing'. We cannot say, without contradiction, that they are simultaneously 'the same sound' and 'not the same sound'. What we will say is that, while they are *phonetically distinct*, they are *phonologically equivalent*. That is, the two types of stop correspond to, are interpreted as belonging to, a single mental category. We will refer to such a category as a **phoneme**. The English speaker interprets the six phonetic segments [p], [pʰ], [t], [tʰ], [k] and [kʰ] in terms of only three phonemes: /p/, /t/ and /k/. We may depict this as follows:

(3)   English voiceless stop phonemes

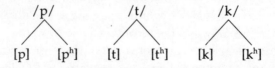

The top line here represents the three voiceless stop phonemes (mental categories) in terms of which the six types of phonetic segment are perceived. The relationship between phonemes and their associated phonetic segments is one of **realization**, so that the phoneme /p/, for instance, is realized as [p] after a voiceless alveolar fricative, and as [pʰ] elsewhere. The most important point is that, on the data we have seen thus far, aspiration or the lack of it is entirely predictable in English: there is a generalization, expressible as a general rule, as to the contexts in which voiceless stops will and will not be aspirated. For most accents of English, this generalization is one that is internalized by children when they acquire English as their native language. The generalization forms part of what native speakers know in knowing their native language, even if that knowledge is largely *unconscious* knowledge. Realizations of a phoneme which are entirely predictable from context are called its **allophones**. We therefore say that [p] and [pʰ] are allophones of the /p/ phoneme in most accents of English. We are claiming that native speakers of English possess phonemes (which are mental categories) and phonological generalizations or rules as part of their (largely unconscious) knowledge of their native language, and that native speakers perceive the allophones they hear in terms of those categories and generalizations.

Compare the English situation with the Korean one. It is clear that the distribution of aspirated and unaspirated voiceless stops in Korean is *overlapping*: there is at least one place (at the beginning of words) in which either type of sound may occur. This kind of distribution is referred to as **parallel distribution**, where 'parallel' means 'overlapping to some degree'.

Furthermore, the distinction between aspirated and unaspirated voiceless stops can make a crucial difference in Korean: when the Korean speaker says [pʰul], it does not mean the same thing as [pul]. The difference between the two sounds is said to be semantically **contrastive**. Pairs of words which differ with respect to only one sound are called **minimal pairs**. Their existence is important, since they demonstrate that the two sounds in question are both in parallel distribution and semantically contrastive.

We therefore want to say that, unlike the English speaker, the Korean perceives the six aspirated and unaspirated voiceless stops [p], [pʰ], [t], [tʰ], [k] and [kʰ] in terms of six different mental categories. That is, [p], for instance, is a realization of the /p/ phoneme, whereas [pʰ] is a realization of a distinct /pʰ/ phoneme. We may depict (part of)[2] the Korean system thus:

(4)   Some Korean voiceless stop phonemes

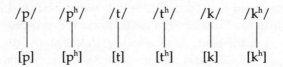

$$/p/ \quad /p^h/ \quad /t/ \quad /t^h/ \quad /k/ \quad /k^h/$$
$$[p] \quad [p^h] \quad [t] \quad [t^h] \quad [k] \quad [k^h]$$

The distinction between aspirated and unaspirated voiceless stops is *phonemic* in Korean but *allophonic* in English. Both English and Korean speakers habitually utter both aspirated and unaspirated voiceless stops. On the phonetic level, the two languages are therefore equivalent as far as bilabial, alveolar and velar voiceless stops are concerned. But at the phonemic level (the mental level), the two languages are quite distinct: the Korean speaker has six mental categories where the English speaker has only three. As far as voiceless stops are concerned, Korean speakers have twice as many phonemic contrasts as English speakers. The difficulty which the English speaker encounters in learning to pronounce and perceive Korean voiceless stops is therefore a *mental* one; it is a *phonological* difficulty, not a purely articulatory one.

This is not to deny that there can be purely articulatory difficulties in learning to speak another language (difficulties in articulating new types of sound which one is not in the habit of articulating). For instance, most speakers of Japanese who are learning to speak English will have to learn to pronounce the sound [l], which they are not in the habit of pronouncing. When learners of a foreign language face this task, they often utter a sound from their native language which is similar to the target sound: in this case, the tap [ɾ] which, like [l], is voiced and alveolar. Similarly, a speaker of French who is trying to master the English sound [ð] will often utter the voiced alveolar fricative [z] or the voiced dental stop [d̪], which she or he is used to uttering in her or his native language. The former is similar to the target sound in being a voiced fricative, while the latter is similar in being a voiced dental sound. Such problems with the pronunciation of foreign languages are widespread. But they are distinct in kind from the kind of problem we have just discussed.

We need not deny either that there may be difficulties in the pronunciation of a foreign language which involve *both* purely articulatory *and* phonological difficulties. For instance, the English speaker who is learning Korean must learn to articulate a third kind of stop which is distinct from voiced stops, aspirated voiceless stops and unaspirated voiceless stops. These are the voiceless stops of Korean which are articulated with 'glottal tension': during their production, the vocal cords do not vibrate, but nor are the vocal cords spread apart, as they are for the voiceless aspirated stops; rather, the vocal cords are constricted.

The English speaker must also learn to (in a sense) *perceive* the distinction between all three sorts of stop in Korean; since the glottally constricted voiceless stops are a new category of sound, they may seem to the English speaker to sound like stops he or she is more used to hearing (voiced stops, for instance). And that is a phonological difficulty, added to the purely articulatory one which the English speaker also has. However, it is clear from the data we have looked at here that there is a type of difficulty which is exclusively phonological, and it is that kind of difficulty which justifies our making a distinction between the kind of articulatory phonetics discussed in the preceding chapters, which constitutes the study of the articulation of speech sounds in and of themselves, and phonology, the study of the system of mental categories in terms of which we interpret those speech sounds.

In examining the phonological differences between Korean and English voiceless stops, we have adopted what is known as **the phonemic principle**, which consists of two sets of two criteria, as follows:

(5)   The phonemic principle

Two or more sounds are realizations of *the same* phoneme if:
(a) they are in complementary distribution

and

(b) they are phonetically similar.
Two or more sounds are realizations of *different* phonemes if:
(a) they are in parallel (overlapping) distribution

and

(b) they serve to signal a semantic contrast.

It is on the basis of the phonemic principle that we say that phonetic differences involving aspiration are allophonic in English but phonemic in Korean.

We have just seen a case where the Korean speaker has more phonemic contrasts than the English speaker. Let us now look at another set of data where the converse is the case. Native speakers of some varieties of Scottish English habitually utter the speech sounds we have represented as '[ɾ]' and '[l]', i.e. the voiced alveolar tap and the voiced lateral alveolar approximant (as in *rip* and *lip*). So do speakers of Korean. Here are some examples of (Scottish) English and Korean words which contain those sounds:

(6) [ɾ] and [l] in Scottish English and Korean

English			*Korean*		
(a)	[læm]	*lamb*	(b)	[mul]	'water'
(c)	[ɾæm]	*ram*	(d)	[mulkama]	'place for water'
(e)	[lɪp]	*lip*	(f)	[muɾe]	'at the water'
(g)	[ɾɪp]	*rip*	(h)	[mal]	'horse'
(i)	[bɛɾi]	*berry*	(j)	[malkama]	'place for horse'
(k)	[bɛli]	*belly*	(l)	[maɾe]	'at the horse'

While speakers of English and Korean habitually utter both sounds, we can predict that many native speakers of Korean who are learning to speak this variety of Scottish English would find the distinction between [l] and [ɾ], when they speak Scottish English, rather difficult to get the hang of. On the face of it, this is puzzling because, as we have just said, Korean speakers have no difficulty in uttering the two sounds, and may well have uttered many thousands of them, long before beginning to learn English. So wherein does the problem reside? One possibility that can be immediately discounted is the suggestion that Korean speakers are encountering some kind of physical, articulatory difficulty: it is clearly *not* the case, as we have seen, that either of the sounds is new to them.

The difficulty is of a *mental* nature, and if one examines the table of data in (6) above, it is clear that, in English, the two sounds may occur in the same places within a word, e.g. at the beginning of words, or between vowels. Furthermore, two words may differ *solely* with respect to the segments [ɾ] and [l]: there are minimal pairs involving

42

The Phonemic Principle

the two sounds ([ɾæm] vs [læm], for instance). In this variety of Scottish English, [ɾ] and [l] are in parallel distribution and can function to signal a semantic contrast. It is important to bear in mind that, when we say that a phonetic difference is contrastive, we refer to a *semantic* contrast, and *not* to a phonetic difference between the sounds.

In Korean, the distinction between [ɾ] and [l] can *never* be contrastive, since [ɾ] and [l] may never occur in the same place. They are in complementary distribution: where one occurs, the other never does, and vice versa. Specifically, [ɾ] in Korean occurs between vowels but nowhere else, whereas [l] *never* occurs between vowels, but may occur elsewhere. Because of this, it is impossible to find minimal pairs involving these two sounds in Korean. The two sounds are also phonetically similar: both are voiced and both entail a closure made between the centre of the tongue blade and the alveolar ridge. Therefore the two sounds are realizations of the same phoneme in Korean.

In this variety of Scottish English, there is a phonemic /ɾ/ vs /l/ contrast. In Korean, on the other hand, there is no such phonemic contrast: whereas this variety of Scottish English has /ɾ/ vs /l/, Korean has only one phoneme: /l/, which has two allophones, [ɾ] and [l]. Put another way, the difference between the sounds [ɾ] and [l] is *phonemic* in English, whereas the difference between [ɾ] and [l] is *allophonic* in Korean. Speakers of this variety of English perceive [ɾ] and [l] in terms of two *distinct* mental categories, whereas Korean speakers perceive them in terms of *a single* mental category. In Korean, the phoneme /l/ is realized as [ɾ] between vowels, and is realized as [l] elsewhere.

We may depict this phonological difference between this variety of Scottish English and Korean as follows:

(7) The phonemic status of [ɾ] and [l] in Scottish English and Korean

	Scottish English speakers	Korean speakers
Phonemic units:	/l/ /ɾ/	/l/
Allophonic units:	[l] [ɾ]	[l] [ɾ]

43

We have now shown where the Korean speakers' difficulty resides: at the level of their (largely) unconscious knowledge of their language. As far as these segments are concerned, Korean and this variety of Scottish English do not differ at the allophonic level: both have [ɾ] and [l]. But they *do* differ at the *phonemic* level: the Scottish English speaker has a mental distinction which the Korean speaker lacks; the Korean speakers' problem is thus *mental* (specifically, perceptual) in nature, not articulatory.

We have said that it is entirely predictable which allophone of the Korean /l/ phoneme will occur in a given context. We may say that there is a **phonological generalization** governing the occurrence of the allophones, which the native speakers of Korean have unconsciously grasped, and which forms part of their linguistic knowledge. We may express that generalization in terms of a **phonological rule**, as follows:

(8) /l/ realization in Korean

/l/ is realized as [ɾ] between vowels.

As we will see, the linguistic knowledge of native speakers contains many such generalizations. As far as [ɾ] and [l] are concerned, the phonological knowledge of the Korean speaker and the Scottish English speaker differ in two respects: (a) the Scottish English speaker has a phonological distinction which the Korean speaker lacks, and (b) the Korean speaker possesses a phonological generalization which the Scottish English speaker lacks. Phonological knowledge consists, therefore, of, among other things, phonological categories and phonological generalizations.

In several varieties of English, the /l/ phoneme also has allophones: 'clear l' ([l]) and 'dark l' ([ɫ]).[3] The following data show the typical distribution of these two sounds in those varieties:

(9) English 'clear l' and 'dark l'

(a)	[kʰlɛvə]	clever	(b) [bɛɫz]	bells
(c)	[pʰleɪn]	plain	(d) [tɹeɪɫ]	trail
(e)	[lʊk]	look	(f) [pʰʊɫ]	pull

44

The Phonemic Principle

(g) [lɔː] law   (h) [bɔːɫz] balls
(i) [laɪ] lie   (j) [pʰaɪɫ] pile

One way of stating the distribution of the allophones is to say that
'clear l' occurs immediately before vowels, whereas 'dark l' occurs
immediately after vowels. We may state the relationship between
the /l/ phoneme and its clear and dark allophones in terms of the
following rule:

(10)   /l/ realization in English

/l/ is realized as [ɫ] immediately after a vowel.

We may depict the realizations of Korean /l/ and /l/ in certain varieties of English as follows:

(11)   /l/ realizations in Korean and English

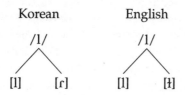

        Korean   English
         /l/   /l/
       /   \   /   \
      [l]   [r]   [l]   [ɫ]

5.3 Phonemes, Allophones and Contexts

We have said that the allophones of a phoneme are predictable realizations of that phoneme. We can predict which allophone will
occur, given a specific context. The sorts of context we have cited
are, in some cases, rather general. For instance, in the Korean data
we considered, we saw that aspirated and unaspirated voiceless stops
may both occur at the beginning of a word. We also saw, in the Korean
data that we looked at, that Korean /l/ is realized as [r] between
vowels. 'At the beginning of a word' and 'between vowels' are quite
general contexts. So is 'at the end of a word', or 'before a consonant',
or 'after a vowel'.

In other cases, the contexts we need to refer to are more specific. For instance, in the English data we looked at, we saw that the unaspirated voiceless stops occurred after a voiceless alveolar fricative. In many cases, there appears to be some kind of phonetic connection between the context in which an allophone occurs and the nature of the allophone itself. Let us consider an example.

In many accents of English, the /ɹ/ phoneme has two realizations: [ɹ] and [ɹ̥] (in which the subscript diacritic denotes voicelessness). The following data exemplify this:[4]

(12)   Voiced and voiceless allophones of /ɹ/ in English

(a)	[tʰɹ̥aɪ]	try	(b)	[əɹeɪ]	array
(c)	[pʰɹ̥uːv]	prove	(d)	[gɹoʊ]	grow
(e)	[kʰɹ̥eɪv]	crave	(f)	[bɹeɪk]	break
(g)	[fɹ̥iː]	free	(h)	[dɹɪŋk]	drink
(i)	[θɹ̥iː]	three	(j)	[bæɹoʊ]	barrow

It is clear that the voiced and voiceless alveolar approximants are in complementary distribution: the voiceless one appears only after voiceless consonants, and the voiced one appears elsewhere. The question is whether we should say that there is a voiced alveolar approximant phoneme which is realized as a voiceless allophone after voiceless consonants, or that there is a voiceless alveolar approximant phoneme which is realized as a voiced approximant after voiced consonants and between vowels. We choose the former claim, since it is more phonetically natural: approximants are normally voiced. Additionally, we can make phonetic sense of the claim that a voiced phoneme has a voiceless realization when it follows voiceless consonants: the realization is assimilating to the preceding segment (it is becoming more like an adjacent segment).

Let us consider another case of this sort. In many accents of English, there are stops which are articulated in front of the velar place of articulation, close to the hard palate. The following data exemplify this ([c] and [ɟ] represent a voiceless and a voiced palatal stop, respectively):

(13) Velar and palatal stops in English

(a) [kʰuːɫ]   cool   (b) [cʰiːp]   keep
(c) [kʰoʊɫ]   coal   (d) [cʰiːn]   keen
(e) [kʰɒp]   cop   (f) [cʰɪt]   kit
(g) [kʰɑːt]   cart   (h) [scɪp]   skip
(i) [guːɫ]   ghoul   (j) [ɟɪə]   gear
(k) [goʊɫ]   goal   (l) [ɟɪɫ]   gill

Once again, the two segment types are in complementary distribution: the advanced, palatal articulations occur before high front vowels, and the velar ones occur elsewhere. We postulate a /k/ phoneme which is 'fundamentally' velar in its place of articulation, but which has a fronted or advanced realization before high front vowels. This makes phonetic sense: high front vowels are palatal articulations (the articulators are the front of the tongue and the hard palate), so we can say that the velar phoneme is assimilating to the following vowel when it is a high front vowel.

We are adopting the view that phonemes often have a kind of 'default' or 'basic' phonetic realization, and that it is this realization which will occur in the absence of specifiable contexts which 'shift' the realization from its default one.

5.4 Summing Up

In this chapter, we have begun to distinguish between phonetics, defined as the study of speech sounds *per se*, and phonology, the study of the system of mental representation, categories and generalizations to which those sounds are related. Native speakers of a language tend to take its phonological system for granted. Speakers of English, for instance, think it perfectly obvious that [ɹ] and [l] are quite distinct, despite the fact that they are, phonetically, very similar. Equally, they cannot easily see that [p] and [pʰ] are different, despite the fact that they are. This chapter has sought to show that what underlies these perceptions is the phonological system of the native language, as distinct from, if intimately related to, the set of speech sounds uttered by native speakers of the language. What sounds one takes to be 'the same' or 'different' depends to a large extent on the system of mental categories which constitutes one's native language phonology. But it is clear that phonetics and phonology are intimately connected.

The extent to which our mentally stored system of language-specific phonological categories governs our perception of a stream of speech sounds was well expressed by the linguist Edward Sapir, who worked with North American Indian languages in the early twentieth century:

> the unschooled recorder of language, provided he has a good ear and a genuine instinct for language, is often at a great advantage as compared with the minute phonetician, who is apt to be swamped by his mass of observations. I have already employed my experience in teaching Indians to write their own language for its testing value in another connection. It yields equally valuable evidence here. I found that it was difficult or impossible to teach an Indian to make phonetic distinctions that did not correspond to 'points in the pattern of his language', however these differences might strike our objective ear, but that subtle, barely audible, phonetic differences, if only they hit the 'points in the pattern', were easily and voluntarily expressed in writing. In watching my Nootka interpreter write his language, I often had the curious feeling that he was transcribing an ideal flow of phonetic elements which he heard, inadequately from a purely objective standpoint, as the intention of the actual rumble of speech.[5] (Sapir 1921: 56)

One can begin to appreciate the extent to which one's native language phonemic categories affect one's perception when one considers that any normal 6-month-old child, no matter what language he or she is beginning to acquire, can distinguish aspirated and unaspirated voiceless stops. Clearly, then, the aspirated/unaspirated difference is one that could in principle act as the basis for a phonemic distinction, and it clearly does act that way in many human languages. But a child who acquires a language (such as most varieties of English) in which the aspirated/unaspirated distinction is allophonic rather than phonemic will come to ignore that distinction at a certain level of awareness. Acquiring the phonology of one's native language can therefore result in a kind of loss of perceptual discrimination, but only at one level of awareness: when a speaker of, say, South African English utters unaspirated stops instead of aspirated stops, this will often be noticed by a speaker of, say, RP, even if the RP speaker notices only that there is something different about the speech of the South African English speaker. Indeed, such differences can be quite striking to the speaker of a language in which unaspirated stops never occur word-initially before a stressed vowel. Such speakers, on being suddenly confronted by English spoken with, say, a Greek accent (on arrival, say, at a Greek airport) will typically think that a word such as *Gatwick* (one of the London airports) is being pronounced as [gadwig]. In cases such as this, the English speaker not only perceives the fact that the stops in question are unaspirated, but also assigns them to the category of English voiced stops, because voiced stops in English are unaspirated, and word-initial and word-final voiced stops in English are barely voiced at all.

Both the native speaker and the adult learner of English can begin to develop an awareness of her or his own phonological system, and of the immense influence this has on one's perception of speech sounds, by comparing and contrasting languages which are phonetically identical (or nearly identical), but phonologically distinct, with respect to some set of sounds. The examples given in this chapter are designed to begin to induce this kind of awareness, as are the exercises which follow.

Notes

1 These data do not show the full range of places in which aspirated and unaspirated voiceless stops occur in most English accents. What we will have to say about their phonological status is therefore very much oversimplified. But the data will suffice to illustrate a valid point.

2 Korean has a third phonemic category of stops, which we discuss below.

3 There are also devoiced allophones of /l/; we ignore these here.

4 We indicate these devoiced sounds here, but henceforth we will not transcribe them using the 'voiceless' diacritic in cases where the devoicing phenomenon is irrelevant to the point being made.

5 Edward Sapir (1921), *Language*, New York: Harcourt Brace, p. 56.

The Phonemic Principle

Exercises

1   [d] and [ð] in English and Spanish

   (a)   English

1.	[dɛn]	den	2. [ðɛn]	then
3.	[douz]	doze	4. [ðouz]	those
5.	[dɛə]	dare	6. [ðɛə]	their
7.	[ʌdə]	udder	8. [ʌðə]	other
9.	[aɪdə]	Eider	10. [aɪðə]	either

In many (not all) accents of English, [d] and [ð] are realizations of *different* phonemes, as these data show. They are in parallel distribution (both occur at the beginnings of words and between vowels). They also function contrastively: there are minimal pairs involving the two sounds. We are therefore justified in postulating a /d/ vs /ð/ phonemic distinction for most accents of English.

(b)   Spanish
Now consider the following Spanish data. (The voiced stop in question is in fact dental in Spanish. We overlook this fact here.) Is the distinction between [d] and [ð] phonemic or allophonic in Spanish? Justify your answer with evidence and argumentation:

1.	[deɾ]	'to give'	2. [neðe]	'nothing'
3.	[deβer]	'to have to'	4. [boðeɣe]	'wine cellar'
5.	[dies]	'days'	6. [ebleðo]	'spoken'
7.	[bende]	'ribbon'	8. [preðo]	'meadow'
9.	[ender]	'to go'	10. [poðer]	'to be able'

2   Voiced stops in English and Korean

In Korean, /p/, /t/ and /k/ have allophones which are unreleased at the end of a word (as can be seen in the data below) or before another consonant. The /p/, /t/ and /k/ phonemes

50

also have voiced stop allophones: [b], [d] and [g]. Unlike English, Korean does not have voiced stop phonemes: [b], [d] and [g] are *always* allophones of /p/, /t/ and /k/ in Korean. Examine the following data and say what contexts the voiced stop allophones occur in:

(a)(i)	[pul]	'fire'	(a)(ii)	[ibul]	'this fire'
(b)(i)	[tal]	'moon'	(b)(ii)	[idal]	'this moon'
(c)(i)	[kan]	'liver'	(c)(ii)	[igan]	'this liver'
(d)(i)	[pap˺]	'cooked rice'	(d)(ii)	[pabi]	'cooked rice' (subject)
(e)(i)	[tat˺]	'close'	(e)(ii)	[tadaɾa]	'close it!'
(f)(i)	[ʧɛk˺]	'book'	(f)(ii)	[ʧɛgi]	'book' (subject)

3 Glottal stops in English and Standard Arabic

The *phonetic* segment [ʔ] (glottal stop) occurs in the speech of most speakers of English, but there is no glottal stop *phoneme* (/ʔ/) in English, since [ʔ] never functions contrastively with any other segment. For instance, [kʰɛʔəɫ] and [kʰɛtəɫ] (*kettle*) are not pronunciations of different words, but different pronunciations of the *same* word. Below are some data from Standard Arabic. Is there a glottal stop phoneme in this language? Explain the reasoning behind your answer:

(a)	[faʔl]	'good fortune'	(b)	[fatl]	'twisting/twining'
(c)	[faʔr]	'rats'	(d)	[faːr]	'it boiled'
(e)	[baʔs]	'strength'	(f)	[baːs]	'he kissed'
(g)	[buʔs]	'misery'	(h)	[buːs]	'bus'

4 Further transcription practice

Transcribe, with as much phonetic detail as possible, the following words as you would utter them in everyday casual speech, paying attention to details such as presence vs absence of aspiration, clear vs dark l, devoiced allophones of /l/ and /ɹ/, and palatal allophones of /k/ and /g/:

started playing price could kill clear creep

6

English Phonemes

6.1 English Consonant Phonemes

We have distinguished phonemes from phonetic segments, and have begun to formulate hypotheses about which phonemes might exist as part of the native speaker's phonological knowledge. Specifically, we have said that many English speakers have the consonant phonemes /l/, /ɹ/, /p/, /t/ and /k/, among others. We will shortly postulate a full system of consonant phonemes which English speakers have. But we must first be a little more precise about what we mean by 'English speakers'. Clearly, there are different varieties of English, which we will be considering in more detail later, and we will need some means of differentiating between them. Let us begin by considering a distinction which is often appealed to by linguists: that between **accent** and **dialect**. It is often said that differences in accent concern solely phonetic and phonological variation, whereas dialect differences involve more than this: they also include differences in vocabulary and syntax. This is a rather simplistic way of putting the distinction, and it is a distinction which is fraught with difficulties, but it will suffice for the present discussion.

We may exemplify the difference between accent and dialect as follows. Perhaps the most widely spoken (and written) English dialect is the 'prestige' dialect known as Standard English, which has its origins in the South East of England; this dialect is used widely, in Britain, in national radio and television, in the press, and indeed in most printed publications. It is possible to speak Standard English *with* a New Zealand accent, a Tyneside accent, a New York City accent, or indeed *any* accent of English. When this happens, we may say (simplifying somewhat) that the speaker is using the vocabulary and syntax of Standard English, while retaining the phonetics and phonology which constitutes the native accent.

Let us exemplify the difference between dialect and accent in a little more detail, as follows. Take the Standard English sentence *You will not be able to put the children on the floor.* Uttered by a speaker with a Standard Scottish English (SSE) accent, the outcome would be:

(1) [jəɬnɒʔbiebɬtəpʰʉʔðə ʧ ɪɫdɹənənðəfloːɹ]

Now compare this with the same Standard English sentence uttered by a speaker of RP. The RP speaker might well utter:

(2) [jəɬnɒʔbieɪbɬtəpʰʊʔðə ʧ ɪɫdɹənənðəflɔː]

Both speakers are speaking Standard English (the syntax is the same, as is the vocabulary, if one excludes the phonological form of the morphemes in that vocabulary), but their accents differ: the SSE speaker's vowel sounds are not always identical to those of the RP speaker, and the SSE speaker utters an [ɹ] in *floor*, which the RP speaker does not.

Now let us imagine that the same SSE speaker wants to convey the same proposition, but speaking, this time, in a dialect other than Standard English: that of Lowland Scots. The result might be:

(3) [jʌɬnoːkɪnpʰɪʔðəbeːɹɪnzonðəfleːʌɹ]

(This might be written as *You'll no can put the bairns on the floor.*)

In (3), the syntax and vocabulary differ from that of Standard English; we may say that these are *dialectal* differences, and distinct in kind from the differences in accent which we noted between (1) and (2) above.

We will return to the matter of accent variation in a later chapter; for the moment, let us look at the consonant phoneme system shared by most varieties of English, which typically looks like this:

(4) English consonant phonemes

/p/	as in *pie, pit, rip*
/b/	as in *buy, bit, rib*
/t/	as in *tie, tip, writ*
/d/	as in *die, dip, rid*
/k/	as in *cool, kit, rick*
/g/	as in *ghoul, git, rig*
/ʧ/	as in *chew, chit, rich*
/ʤ/	as in *Jew, gin, ridge*
/θ/	as in *thigh, thin, with*
/ð/	as in *then, that, scythe*
/f/	as in *fie, fit, riff*
/v/	as in *Venn, vat, leave*
/s/	as in *sigh, sit, lease*
/z/	as in *zoo, zip, please*
/h/	as in *high, hip*
/ʃ/	as in *shy, ship, leash, mesher*
/ʒ/	as in *measure*
/w/	as in *wet, win*
/l/	as in *lie, lip, real*
/ɹ/	as in *rye, rip*
/j/	as in *year*
/m/	as in *my, meat, rim*
/n/	as in *nigh, neat, sin*
/ŋ/	as in *sing, ring*

The evidence comes partly in the form of the sorts of minimal pair cited in (4), such as *measure/mesher* ([mɛʒə]/[mɛʃə]) and *sigh/shy* ([saɪ]/[ʃaɪ]), but we have by no means presented all of the evidence here. Let us look briefly at some of the evidence for the three nasal stop phonemes postulated here:

(5) Evidence for English nasal stop phonemes

(a)	[mi:t]	'meat'	(b)	[ni:t]	'neat'
(c)	[moʊɫ]	'mole'	(d)	[noʊɫ]	'knoll'
(e)	[sɪn]	'sin'	(f)	[sɪŋ]	'sing'

(g) [dɪm] 'dim'   (h) [dɪn] 'din'
(i) [wɪn] 'win'   (j) [wɪŋ] 'wing'

It is clear that [m] and [n] are in parallel distribution: each may occur word-initially or word-finally. The distinction is also contrastive: it forms the basis for minimal pairs such as *meat/neat*. It is also clear that [n] and [ŋ] are in parallel distribution: while [ŋ] does not appear in word-initial position, both may occur in word-final position. The distinction is also contrastive, as is shown by the existence of minimal pairs such as *win/wing*. The distinction between [m] and [ŋ] is contrastive too, as pairs such as *whim/wing* show. We therefore have clear evidence for a three-way phonemic distinction between /m/, /n/ and /ŋ/. We will consider this analysis in more detail below. The main point to be made at the moment is that we postulate the existence of phonemes on the basis of evidence and argumentation; if phonemes are perceptual categories, they cannot be directly observed.

6.2 The Phonological Form of Morphemes

We have said that, in knowing a language, a speaker possesses largely unconscious linguistic knowledge, which subsumes semantic, syntactic and phonological knowledge. And we have said that the phonological units or categories we have called phonemes are part of that phonological knowledge. As we progress in this book, we will investigate the question of what other sorts of phonological knowledge speakers possess, besides phonemes alone. Let us begin this investigation by considering the internal structure of words. You will agree that the English word *cats* may be broken down into two component parts. Let us call those component parts **morphemes**. Then we may say that this word consists of a **root** morpheme and a plural morpheme (which, in this case, is a **suffix**). Let us say that words of this sort are **morphologically complex**: they consist of more than one morpheme. Let us say that a morpheme takes the form of a triple: a syntax, a semantics and a phonology. Take the morpheme *cat*: it has a syntax (it is a noun), a semantics (it means 'cat') and a phonology, which takes the form /kæt/; we will refer to this as the

phonological form of the morpheme. The phonological form of a morpheme may, clearly, consist of more than one phoneme. Just as phonemes are mental objects, so the phonological form of this morpheme is a mental object: /kæt/ is a *mental representation* in the mind of a speaker, whereas the sequence [kʰæt] is a *phonetic* sequence.

Let us now consider the adjectives *impossible, imbalanced, infelicitous, intangible, indirect, insane, incorrect* and *inglorious*. All consist of at least a **prefix** morpheme and a root morpheme (some of these words have a prefix, a root *and* a suffix). Many speakers have the following pronunciations of these words:

(6) (a) [ɪmpʰɒsɪbł]   impossible
     (b) [ɪmbælənst]   imbalanced
     (c) [ɪɱfəlɪsɪtəs]   infelicitous
     (d) [ɪntʰændʒɪbł]   intangible
     (e) [ɪndɪɹɛkt]   indirect
     (f) [ɪnseɪn]   insane
     (g) [ɪŋkəɹɛkt]   incorrect
     (h) [ɪŋglɔːɹɪəs]   inglorious

It is part of the native speaker's unconscious linguistic knowledge of English that these words all have the *same* prefix. That prefix is one of the morphemes of English, and, like all morphemes in the language, has a syntax (it is a prefix), a semantics (it has a specific meaning) and a phonology. But what *is* the phonological form of that morpheme? We know from the data that the suffix may be realized as [ɪm], [ɪɱ], [ɪn] or [ɪŋ]. It is clear, then, that the first phoneme in the prefix is /ɪ/ and the second phoneme is a nasal, but *which* nasal phoneme? We claimed above that English has three nasal phonemes: /m/, /n/ and /ŋ/. So the phonological form of this prefix might be /ɪm/, /ɪn/ or /ɪŋ/. Let us consider /ɪŋ/. We could say that the /ŋ/ phoneme is realized as [n] before /t/, /d/ and /s/, and as [m] before [p] and [b]. This seems to make sense: we can say that, when the prefix is added to a root, the place of articulation of the nasal becomes identical to that of the first consonant in the root. Thus, it is alveolar when followed by an alveolar consonant (such as /t/, /d/ and /s/), labio-dental when followed by a labio-dental consonant (such as /f/), and bilabial when followed by a bilabial consonant (such as /p/ or /b/). This is the process of assimilation we referred to in chapter 2, in which one segment becomes similar, in some respect, to another when the two are adjacent. Here, the assimilation is in place of articulation. Further evidence that nasals in English undergo place of articulation assimilation is not hard to come by. Consider the following data, which are representative of the speech of many speakers of English:

(7) Nasal assimilation in English

(a)	[ʌŋkʰlɪə]	'unclear'	(b)	[ʌŋgɒdli]	'ungodly'
(c)	[ʌmɛə]	'unfair'	(d)	[ʌɱvælju:d]	'unvalued'
(e)	[ʌntʰɹu:]	'untrue'	(f)	[ʌndʌn]	'undone'
(g)	[ʌmbɛəɹəbəɫ]	'unbearable'	(h)	[ʌmbaɪəst]	'unbiased

While the /ɪŋ/ solution is plausible, it faces a difficulty: we might equally say that the phonological form of the morpheme is /ɪn/, or /ɪm/, and that, in either case, the nasal assimilates to a following consonant. On the evidence presented thus far, there is no non-arbitrary way of choosing between the three alternatives: each is as plausible as the others. The following data, however, allow us to make a non-arbitrary choice:

(8) (a) [ɪnæktɪv]   'inactive'
     (b) [ɪnɒpɹətɪv]   'inoperative'
     (c) [ɪnɛfəbɫ]   'ineffable'
     (d) [ɪnədvaɪzəbɫ]   'inadvisable'
     (e) [ɪnɔ:dɪbɫ]   'inaudible'
     (f) [ɪneɪliənəbɫ]   'inalienable'

In each case, there is no consonant at the beginning of the root to which the nasal *could* assimilate: each root begins with a vowel. From the fact that vowel-initial roots are realized with the [ɪn] form, we can therefore conclude that the phonology of the prefix takes the form /ɪn/, and that the nasal does not change its place of articulation if the root-initial segment is a vowel or an alveolar consonant. Note that this is generally true of alveolar nasals in English, as the following data, involving the prefix seen in (7), suggests:

(9) (a) [ʌneɪdəd]   'unaided'
     (b) [ʌnətʰɹæktɪv]   'unattractive'
     (c) [ʌnivɛntfəł]   'uneventful'
     (d) [ʌnɔ:θədɒks]   'unorthodox'

We might, of course, have said that the morpheme in question has *four different phonological forms*: /ɪm, /ɪŋ/, /ɪn/ and /ɪŋ/, and that words such as *impossible, infelicitous, indirect* and *incorrect* are each stored mentally with the appropriate prefix. There are two problems with this approach. Firstly, there is no independent evidence that there is an /ŋ/ phoneme in English ([ŋ] never functions contrastively with any other nasal). Secondly, even if there were no [ɪŋ] forms, we would be committed to claiming, under the 'several phonological forms' approach, that it is *mere coincidence* that the /ɪm/ form is attached *only* to roots beginning with a bilabial consonant, the /ɪŋ/ form only to roots beginning with a velar consonant, and the /ɪn/ form only to roots beginning with alveolar consonants and vowels. But that is surely an implausible claim. So, for this sort of case at least, the idea that we should postulate more than one phonological form for a morpheme is deeply unattractive and implausible. Given the data we have seen thus far, it appears much more plausible to say that any given morpheme has a single phonological form. And if that is the case, then it is the phonologist's task to hypothesize as to what that form might be. In doing so, she or he will be guided by *evidence and argumentation*: the facts of the matter, since they are mental in nature, and thus not directly observable, will not be available for immediate inspection via the five senses.

In adopting this 'one phonological form per morpheme' approach, we are allowing that, while any given morpheme has only one phonological form, that phonological form may 'correspond' in some sense to a variety of different phonetic forms. In the case we have just looked at, the prefix has the phonological form /ɪn/, but that in turn corresponds to four different phonetic forms: [ɪm], [ɪŋ], [ɪn] and [ɪŋ]. Phonologists refer to such phonetic forms as **alternants**: we say that there is an **alternation** between the four forms. Which alternant of a given morpheme occurs in a given word is entirely *predictable*; there is a generalization which captures that predictability, and we are able to express it in the form of a phonological rule, just as we did with [ɾ] and [l] in Korean. In our English case, the rule in question concerns nasals in general; it might be put informally as:

(10)   The rule of nasal assimilation in English

If the phonological form of a prefix ends in a nasal then that nasal will assimilate to the place of articulation of a following consonant.

We could have formulated this generalization as a formalized rule, or as some kind of constraint on the phonological form of morphemes in English. We will not go into the types of formalism required to express such generalizations, or inquire whether they are best expressed as rules or as constraints. The most important point is that native speakers appear to be in possession of generalizations of this sort, and that these appear to constitute a part of their largely unconscious phonological knowledge.

The data we have just considered also exemplify an important phenomenon: that of **phonemic overlapping**. On the basis of the data in (5), we postulated the following nasal stop phonemes, with the realizations shown:

(11)   /m/   /n/   /ŋ/
                         ↓   ↓   ↓
                        [m]   [n]   [ŋ]

However, we have allowed that the /n/ phoneme may also be realized as [m] if it precedes a bilabial consonant, or [ŋ] if it precedes a velar consonant. This means that a given occurrence of [m], for instance, may be either a realization of /m/, as in *map*, or a realization of /n/, as in *improbable*. That is, the /m/ and /n/ phonemes *overlap* in their realizations. We may depict this as follows:

(12)   /m/   /n/   /ŋ/
                         ↓⤡   ⤢↓⤡   ⤢↓
                        [m]   [n]   [ŋ]

59

The question arises: how can the speaker of English tell whether a given [m] is a realization of /m/ or of /n/? The answer is that the phonological context allows the speaker to tell: an [m] which does *not* precede a bilabial consonant will be a realization of the /m/ phoneme.

6.3 English Vowel Phonemes

Accents of English vary considerably in their vowel phoneme systems and in the range of allophones that those phonemes have. We begin by depicting a set of postulated vowel phonemes for RP and GA. The RP and GA phonetic vowel qualities we presented and discussed in chapters 3 and 4 are typically contrastive for most speakers of those accents, and we may therefore postulate the following (stressed) vowel phonemes for RP and GA:

(13a)	RP vowel phonemes		(13b)	GA vowel phonemes
/ʌ/	as in *putt*		/ʌ/	as in *putt*
/ʊ/	as in *put*		/ʊ/	as in *put*
/uː/	as in *pool, shoe*		/uː/	as in *pool, shoe*
/ɪ/	as in *pit*		/ɪ/	as in *pit*
/iː/	as in *peat, lea*		/iː/	as in *peat, lea*
/ɛ/	as in *pet*		/ɛ/	as in *pet*
/eɪ/	as in *pate, lay*		/eɪ/	as in *pate, lay*
/ɒ/	as in *pot*			
/oʊ/	as in *pole, low*		/oʊ/	as in *pole, low*
/ɔː/	as in *port, law*		/ɔː/	as in *law, short, caught*
/æ/	as in *pat*		/æ/	as in *pat*
/ɑː/	as in *part, Shah*		/ɑ/	as in *part, Shah, pot*
/ɜː/	as in *pert, furry*		/ɜ/	as in *pert, furry*
/ɔɪ/	as in *coin, boy*		/ɔɪ/	as in *coin, boy*
/aɪ/	as in *pile, buy*		/aɪ/	as in *pile, buy*
/aʊ/	as in *pout, cow*		/aʊ/	as in *pout, cow*
/ɪə/	as in *fierce, leer*			
/ɛə/	as in *scarce, lair*			
/ʊə/	as in *gourd, lure*			

Again, what the set of RP or GA vowel phonemes might be is a matter for argumentation based on evidence and general theoretical considerations. For instance, we might have suggested that the second vowel in words like *pew* is a diphthong ([iu:]) and that, since *pew* forms a minimal pair with *pie*, *pea*, etc., then /iu:/ is an RP vowel phoneme. We will return, in due course, to this kind of question. We should also note that there is a further vowel phoneme which is not listed here: /ə/ (schwa), which differs from all the other phonemes listed above, since it does not occur in stressed position (as we noted in chapter 3). We will also return, in due course, to /ə/ and its relation to the phonetic segment [ə].

Like consonant phonemes, vowel phonemes may have allophones. For instance, speakers of many accents of English have two realizations of the vowel phoneme /i:/: [i:] and [i:ə]. The latter typically occurs before a velarized lateral ('dark l'), as the following data show:

(14) Allophones of /i:/

(a) [fi:t]   feet   (b) [fi:əɫ]   feel
(c) [di:p]   deep   (d) [di:əɫ]   deal
(e) [pʰi:k]   peak   (f) [pʰi:əɫ]   peel
(g) [si:m]   seem   (h) [si:əɫ]   seal

We postulate /i:/ rather than /i:ə/ as the form of the phoneme, since we assume that the realization of the phoneme when it precedes a dark l is influenced by the dark l. The schwa articulation, which is retracted from the high front [i:] position, is a matter of the vowel articulation assimilating to the tongue body retraction in the dark l. In doing so, we appeal to the idea of **phonetic motivation**: our analysis is phonetically motivated in the sense that we can provide an articulatory reason for the /i:/ → [i:ə] process, whereas we would be unable to provide any such motivation for a process in which /i:ə/ → [i:] word-finally and before any consonant other than [ɫ].

We are also assuming, as we did in chapter 5, that the phoneme /l/ has two allophones, [l] and [ɫ]. We said there that there is an /l/ realization rule: /l/ is realized as [l] immediately *before* vowels, and as [ɫ] immediately *after* vowels.

does not contain any consonants in coda position is referred to as an **open syllable**; as in the word *buy*:

(2) *buy*:

While a syllable *must* have a nucleus, it is possible to have a well-formed syllable which does not contain any element other than a nucleus. The segment occupying the nucleus of the syllable is norm-ally a vowel. An example of a word in English consisting of only one syllable, which in turn contains only a nucleus, is *eye*: /aɪ/. But the nucleus of a syllable in English may be preceded or followed by other segments, as we have seen, and those segments are typically consonants. In the word *aisle*, for instance, the nucleus is followed by a consonant in coda position: /aɪl/. In the word *buy*, the nucleus is preceded by a consonant in onset position: /baɪ/, and in the word *bile*, the nucleus is both preceded and followed by consonants: /baɪl/.

Morphemes like *bile*, which contain only one syllable, are said to be **monosyllabic**. In some languages, *all* morphemes are monosyl-labic. But in English, morphemes may contain more than one syl-lable: they may be **polysyllabic**. Examples are *rider, beetle, amount, desire* (which are bisyllabic), *elephant, veranda, kangaroo* (which are tri-syllabic), *independent, America* (which have four syllables) and so on.

In some languages, all syllables *must* contain an onset consonant but, as we have seen, in English (and this is true of many other lan-guages), this is not the case. For reasons to be explained later (con-nected with the notion of 'resyllabification'), we will represent such syllables with an **empty onset**, as follows:

(3) *it*:

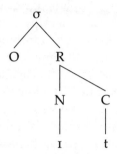

In many languages, such as Hawaiian, onsets may contain a single consonant only, but in many others, English included, onsets may contain two segments (as in *bring, trap, clip,* etc.); we will refer to these as **branching onsets**, and represent them as follows:

(4) *clip*:

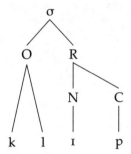

Just as onsets may be branching, so codas may branch, as in the word *hunt*:

(5) *hunt*:

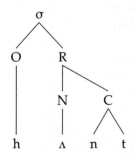

The distinction between, on the one hand, short vowels and, on the other, long vowels and diphthongs can be represented by taking the latter class of vowels to occupy a **branching nucleus**, with the former class occupying a non-branching nucleus. To represent the fact that long vowels and diphthongs are longer than short vowels, we say that segments are attached to a series of *timing slots*, referred to as the **skeletal tier**. The idea is that one can represent the difference between short vowels on the one hand, and long vowels (including English diphthongs) on the other, by taking the former to be connected to a single skeletal slot and the latter to be connected to two skeletal slots. Thus, *bit* has a short vowel as its nucleus and is therefore represented with a non-branching nucleus, whereas *bee* and *buy* have branching nuclei:

(6) *bit*:

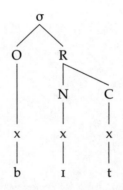

(7) *bee*:

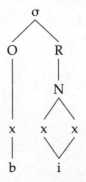

(8) *buy*:

What is intended by the representations in (7) and (8) is that long vowels are constituted as a single vowel quality which is attached to two skeletal slots, whereas long diphthongs, as in *buy*, have two different vowel qualities. The point is that nuclei with long vowels and with diphthongs are parallel with respect to the number of timing slots within the nucleus. We will henceforth adopt the skeletal tier in our representations of syllabic structure.

The skeletal tier enables us to say that affricates, which, as we have seen, have a closure element and a fricative release element, as in [tʃ] and [ʤ], are **complex segments**, since they behave like single segments (they occupy a single unit of timing) while having an internal structure which resembles two segments:

(9) *chip*:

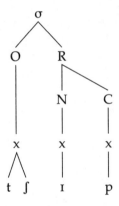

7.3 The Sonority Hierarchy, Maximal Onset and Syllable Weight

You will agree, if you are a native speaker of English, that /blɪŋk/ is a well-formed syllable (and happens to constitute the phonological form of an English word), as are the following: /blʊŋk/, /blɛŋk/, /blɒŋk/ and /blæŋk/ (most of which happen not to constitute the phonological form of English words). That is, your native speaker knowledge of English allows you to judge that these are syllabically well-formed, even though there are no words in English which have those phonological forms. That unconscious knowledge also allows you to judge that the following are ill-formed: /lbɪŋk/, /lbɪkŋ/, /tlɪnk/ and /blaɪmp/. The question is: what form does this unconscious knowledge take? What is it that we know, unconsciously, which allows us to make these judgements? Let us now seek to answer that question.

It is widely believed that there are both **universal** and **language-specific** constraints on the form that syllables may take, that is, constraints on the **syllabification** of sequences of segments. Among the universal constraints, we may mention two. Firstly, it is claimed that sequences of segments are syllabified in accordance with a **sonority scale**, which takes the following form:

(10)   Sonority scale

Low vowels
High vowels
Approximants
Nasals
Voiced fricatives
Voiceless fricatives
Voiced stops
Voiceless stops

The idea is that, as one proceeds from the bottom to the top of the scale, the class of segments becomes more sonorous, or more vowel-like. Sonority is an acoustic effect: the more sonorous a sound, the more it resonates. Vowels have greater resonance than consonants, and voiced consonants have greater resonance than voiceless ones. If you listen to a singer holding a note for any length of time, the sound in question will most probably be a vowel. There are two articulatory reasons why it is easier to hold a vowel sound for longer than a consonant sound, and both are relevant to the production of sonority. The first is *degree of constriction*, as discussed in chapter 1, whereby stops are said to involve a greater degree of stricture than fricatives, which in turn involve greater constriction than

approximants and vowels. Similarly, the more open a vowel articulation, the less stricture there is in the oral cavity. The acoustic effect
of these sorts of articulation is that the lesser the degree of constriction, the greater the degree of sonority. The second articulatory factor
is *voicing*: voiceless segments are less vowel-like, less sonorant, than
voiced segments: vowels are typically voiced, and voicing creates
greater sonority.

Applied to syllable structure, the idea is that the most sonorous
element in a syllable will be located within the nucleus, and that,
the further one gets from the nucleus, the less sonorous are the segments. Thus, in *blink*, the /b/ is less sonorous than the /l/, which
is, in turn, less sonorous than the vowel: as one approaches the
nucleus, so sonority increases. As one leaves the nucleus, we may
note that the /ŋ/ is less sonorous than the vowel, and the /k/ less
sonorous in turn than the preceding /ŋ/.

The 'degree of sonority' idea is very convincing, even if it runs
into some difficulties. For instance, [s] + consonant onset clusters in
English undermine the predictions made by the sonority hierarchy,
since, in cases such as *sprint*, the sonority scale principle makes the
right predictions except with respect to the initial [s]. However,
this merely serves further to underline the peculiarity of English sC
(s + consonant) onset clusters: only [s]-initial onsets violate the
sonority hierarchy, and the only three-way branching onsets in
English are those which begin with an [s].

Another universal principle of syllabification concerns the syllabification of polysyllabic words, and is referred to as the principle
of **Maximal Onset**. We have considered only monosyllabic words
thus far; let us therefore consider the syllabification of the English
word *appraise*, whose segmental form is, let us say, /əpɹeɪz/. It is
clear that the word is bisyllabic; the question is where the boundary between the syllables lies. We know that /p/ may occur in
coda position in English, as in *cap, cup*, etc. We also know that /pɹ/
is a well-formed onset, as in *prize, preen*, etc., and we know that /ɹ/
may occur alone in onset position, as in *rice, raze*, etc. Furthermore,
we know that /pɹ/ is not a well-formed coda cluster: it violates the
predictions of the sonority hierarchy. Thus, /uːpɹ/, /sɪpɹ/, etc. are
ill-formed. We must therefore decide whether the syllabification

of *appraise* is /ə.pɹeɪz/, or /əp.ɹeɪz/ (where the full stop indicates the syllable boundary). The principle of Maximal Onset says that, in cases like this, where the language-specific phonotactics will allow for two or more syllabifications across a syllable boundary, it is the syllabification which maximizes the material in the following onset which is preferred. In this case, that is the former syllabification.

The principle of Maximal Onset is intimately connected with a universal fact about syllable structure: that syllables with an onset consonant are in some sense more basic than those without, and that presence of onset consonants is in some sense more basic than presence of coda consonants. It appears that the most 'basic' syllable structure in human languages is CV syllable structure, with a single onset consonant followed by a vowel. There are several types of evidence for this claim.

Firstly, CV-type syllables appear to be the syllable types that human children first utter when they begin to speak (e.g. [ba], [ma]) regardless of what language their parents speak. At that stage in the development of the child's syllable structure, syllables in the adult language with branching onsets will be uttered as CV structures. So too will syllables with coda consonants: the coda consonants will simply be absent at that stage. This strongly suggests that onset consonants are in some way more basic, in articulatory, and perhaps perceptual, terms than coda consonants.

Secondly, in many cases of aphasia, where post-stroke patients have suffered damage to their speech, CV syllable structures also appear to be the sort that first begins to appear as the patient recovers his or her speech, even if his or her native language has branching onsets and coda consonants.

Thirdly, languages which have both onset and coda consonants typically allow for a wider range of consonants to occur in onset position than in coda position.

Fourthly, coda consonants are much more likely to undergo loss of articulation in the course of the historical development of languages than onset consonants. This is what has happened with /l/ in coda position in some varieties of English, where the realization of /l/ has become vocalized ([w], which is vowel-like, rather than consonantal) in coda position, but not in onset position, so that [l] occurs in words like *let* and *play*, where the /l/ is in an onset, but [w] occurs in words like *feel* and *felt*, where the /l/ occurs in coda position (except in cases where words such as *feel* are followed by a word or suffix beginning with an empty onset, in which case the /l/ occupies that position and is realized as [l]; see 7.7 below on resyllabification). This kind of weakening of articulation can lead to complete **elision** (non-pronunciation) of a consonant. This is what has happened with [ɹ] in coda position in many accents of English. In those accents, words like *car* and *card* have lost the coda [ɹ], while retaining it in onsets, as in words like *run* and *bring*.

Such cases of articulatory weakening, often leading to complete loss of articulation, of coda consonants abound in the world's languages. They suggest that coda consonants are somehow less salient in perception than onset consonants, and studies in the way that human beings retrieve phonological forms from mental storage suggest greater prominence for onset consonants than for coda consonants: if one is searching for a word in one's lexical memory, one is more likely to search on the basis of onset consonants than of coda consonants.

Fifthly, there are no known languages which have VC-type syllables but lack CV-type syllables, whereas the reverse is not the case. This strongly suggests that CV syllables are more basic than VC, or indeed any other, syllable type.

This generalization about CV syllable structure probably has a basis in both articulation and perception. If you try to produce a word with an empty onset in isolation (e.g. the word *eye*), you will find it hard to do without uttering some kind of consonantal articulation (typically, a glottal stop) before you utter the vowel. Preference for filled, rather than empty, onsets is probably rooted in the nature of our articulatory apparatus and also tied to greater perceptual salience of onset consonants.

Given the principle of Maximal Onset, it is clear that, in a syllable such as the first syllable in *appraise*, the rhyme contains a short vowel (dominated, of course, by a single skeletal slot) and does not contain a coda, thus:

(11) *appraise*:

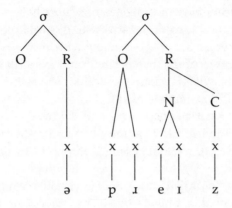

Syllables such as the first syllable in *appraise*, in which there is no branching within the rhyme, either at the level of the rhyme node itself, or within the nucleus, are called **light syllables**. And syllables which have branching anywhere within the rhyme constituent are called **heavy syllables**. This distinction in **syllable weight** is important in understanding the nature of word stress in English; which we will examine shortly.

There are two generalizations about word stress in English which we can make at this stage. The first is that any stressed syllable in English is very likely to be a heavy syllable. The second is that monosyllabic words may not end in one of the short vowel phonemes (/ɪ/, /ɪ/, /æ/, /ɛ/, /ɒ/ or /ʌ/), since a nucleus containing only one of those vowels, with no coda consonant, is light, and if a monosyllabic word is to be stressed, there is no choice as to which syllable it will be stressed on.

7.4 Language-Specific Phonotactics

Let us now consider some language-specific constraints on the sequences of segments which may be combined in syllable structure, known as language-specific **phonotactic constraints** (phonotactics, for short).

We have allowed that, in English syllables, onsets, nuclei, rhymes and codas may branch. But we have not said whether there is any *limit* on the number of branches they may have. Only one sort of English onset exceeds binary (two-way) branching: /s/ + consonant + {/j/, /w/ or /ɹ/} onsets, as in *spew, square* and *scream.* Note that the range of segments which may form the third element in such sequences is even more restricted than those in binary branching onsets.

As we have seen, onsets may branch in English, but if they do, there are phonotactic constraints on the form they may take. Ignoring the /s/ + consonant cases, we may say that the first segment must be a stop or a fricative and the second must be /ɹ/, /l/, /j/ or /w/. Thus /pɹ/, /pl/, /pj/, /bɹ/, /bl/, /bj/, /tɹ/, /tw/, /dɹ/, /dw/, /kɹ/, /kl/, /kw/, /θɹ/, /θw/, /fɹ/, /fl/, /fj/, /sl/, /sj/ and /sw/ are all permissible. This list reflects other onset phonotactics. For instance, /t/, /d/ and /θ/ may not be followed by /l/, and none of the voiced fricatives may occur in branching onsets.

Among the phonotactic constraints on rhymes in English, we may note the following. Firstly, /h/ does not occur in rhymes in English. Secondly, in many accents of English, /ɹ/ does not occur in rhymes either; so that words like *farm* and *car* arguably have phonological forms such as /fɑːm/ and /kɑː/, without an /ɹ/. Accents which lack /ɹ/ in rhymes are referred to as **non-rhotic** accents; they include Australian English, New Zealand English, RP, South African English, most of the accents of the North of England, and the Southern and Eastern accents of the United States. These accents were rhotic at one stage; [ɹ] has been lost in rhymes in those accents. Rhotic accents, which have not undergone this historical change, include GA, the accents of English spoken in Scotland, and some accents spoken in the South West of England. We will discuss such accents in more detail later.

The overall shape of syllables in a language often acts as a major factor in adult second language acquisition. For instance, simplifying somewhat, Japanese syllable structure does not allow for branching onsets. This often has the effect that, when native speakers of Japanese utter English words with complex onsets, such as *screw*, they will tend to insert a vowel after each of the first three consonants, thus rendering the word trisyllabic: [sɯkɯɾɯ]. This process of vowel insertion is known as vowel **epenthesis**, and such vowels are known as epenthetic vowels. Similarly, and again simplifying somewhat, Japanese syllable structure does not allow for word-final coda consonants, so that English loanwords, such as *cake*, which end in a coda consonant in English, tend to be uttered as bisyllabic words ending in a vowel: [keki].

Similar cases abound. For instance, Spanish, unlike English, does not have words beginning with an s + consonant onset. However, Spanish does have words such as *España* which, in some cases, correspond to English words with an s + consonant onset (in this case, the word *Spain*). One of the effects of this is that Spanish speakers tend to insert an [ɛ] before English words beginning with s + consonant clusters, as in [ɛspeɪn] (*Spain*). Similarly, English loanwords in Spanish are pronounced with such an epenthetic [ɛ], as in [ɛsmokin] ('smoking jacket').

7.5 Syllabic Consonants and Phonotactics

It is possible for consonants to form the nucleus of a syllable in the speech of English speakers, particularly as the rate of speech increases. These consonants are called **syllabic consonants**. Three alternative pronunciations of the word *bottle*, for many speakers, are [bɒtəɫ], [bɒtɫ̩] or [bɒʔɫ̩]. In the latter two pronunciations, the final unstressed vowel (schwa) has been lost, but the word still has two syllables, with the lateral becoming syllabified. Syllabic consonants are transcribed by means of the 'syllabic' diacritic, placed under the appropriate consonant symbol.

Syllabic nasals are common in many varieties of English. An example is the word *button*, which has two syllables. For many speakers of English, it may be pronounced [bʌtən] or [bʌʔn̩], where the second pronunciation has a syllabic nasal. The second vowel in the first pronunciation is an unstressed vowel (schwa) which may be 'lost', particularly in faster or more casual speech. A similar example is the word *happen*, which, for many speakers, has (at least) the two pronunciations [hæpən] and [hæʔm̩]. Here, the nasal [n] assimilates to the 'intended' bilabial articulation [p], which in turn is articulated as a glottal stop. Other examples involving nasals are [ɹɛʔŋ̩] vs [ɹɛkən] (*reckon*), and [kn̩u:] vs [kənu:] (*canoe*).

A similar example involving the approximant [ɹ] is the word *parade*, which often has the alternative pronunciations [pəɹeɪd] and [pɹ̩eɪd]. It is typically nasals, laterals and [ɹ] which undergo syllabification in English, although fricatives may also be syllabified, as in some pronunciations of, for instance, *support*, which may be [səpʰɔːt] or [sp̩ʰɔːt] (as distinct from *sport*: [spɔːt], with one, not two, syllables).

In English (but not in some other languages), for every case in which a syllabic consonant may occur, there will be an alternative pronunciation of the word with a vowel preceding or following the syllabified consonant.

All of these words have phonological representations containing a vowel in the nucleus of each syllable, as in *canoe*:

(12) *canoe*:

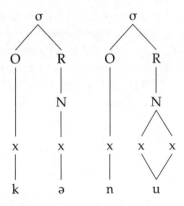

It is striking that, although English speakers frequently utter words such as *canoe* with a syllabic nasal, as in [knu:], when faced with non-English words such as *gnu*, they will tend to insert an epenthetic vowel, uttering the word as [gənu:], making it conform to English syllable structure, in which /gn/ is not an English onset. The important point to be made here is that constraints on English syllable structure are defined in terms of permissible *phonological* sequences, rather than *phonetic* ones.

We have said that English does not allow for phonological syllabic consonants, but many other languages do. The Polynesian language Maori, and many Bantu languages, for instance, allow for phonologically syllabic nasals. Examples are Bantu names such as *Mbabande, Ndola* and *Nkomo*, each of which begins, phonologically, with a syllabic nasal, as in [ŋkomo], which has three syllables. Native speakers of English will tend to utter such words with an epenthetic vowel placed adjacent to the relevant nasal, as in [nɪkomo] or [ɪŋkomo], thus making the phonetic sequence conform to the English phonological pattern. All of these cases provide evidence for the phonological vs phonetic distinction we have drawn, and show how profound an influence our phonological representations can have on our perception and production of non-native words.

7.6   Syllable-Based Generalizations

We said in 7.1 that some of the evidence for the existence of the syllable as a phonological constituent comes from the fact that there are significant phonological generalizations which cannot be adequately expressed without appeal to syllable structure. One such generalization concerns the distribution of velarized laterals ('dark l's) in many accents of English. For many speakers, the following sort of distribution between velarized and non-velarized /l/ may be found:

(13)   Velarized and non-velarized /l/

[lʌɫ]	lull	[li:f]	leaf	[sli:p]	sleep
[bɒtɫ]	bottle	[pi:əɫ]	peel	[mɪɫk]	milk
[lɪli]	lilly	[lɪɫtɪŋ]	lilting	[fɑ:ɫtə]	falter

One might attempt to state the distribution of [l] and [ɫ] as follows: [ɫ] occurs when immediately followed by another consonant, or at the end of a word (i.e. when immediately followed by a word boundary). But one of the objections to this formulation is that it is not clear what, if anything, a following consonant and a word boundary might have in common. A simpler statement of the distribution, which does not entail appeal to this peculiar disjunction of environments, is to say that [ɫ] occurs in the *rhyme* of a syllable, and [l] in the *onset*. Indeed, we might take that syllable-based account of the distribution to help us diagnose the syllabic status of the second /l/ in *lily*: we might say that, because the second /l/ is not velarized in the speech of many speakers, this confirms our claim that it occupies onset position in the second syllable of *lily*, rather than coda position in the first syllable.

Let us consider another example, from London English, of the syllable-based nature of some phonological generalizations. The vowels [ɒʊ] and [ʌʊ] are said by some phonologists to be in complementary distribution in the speech of many speakers of London English. The following table exemplifies this:

(14) [ɒʊ] and [ʌʊ] in London English

[ɹɒʊl]	roll	[kʌʊlʌ]	cola
[stɹɒʊl]	stroll	[lʌʊd]	load
[ɒʊld]	old	[tɒmbʌʊlʌ]	tombola

The claim is that the /ʌʊ/ phoneme is realized as [ɒʊ] when it is followed by an /l/ which is in the same syllable as the /ʌʊ/ (i.e. when followed by a **tautosyllabic** /l/), and as [ʌʊ] elsewhere. Thus, in the words in the left-hand column, we have [ɒʊ]. In the right-hand column, the vowel in *load* clearly lacks a following tautosyllabic /l/; as for *cola* and *tombola*, we would want to argue, from the principle of Maximal Onset, that the /l/s there occupy onset position in the following syllable, and thus that the /ʌʊ/ there also lacks a following tautosyllabic /l/.

7.7 Morphological Structure, Syllable Structure and Resyllabification

The case just cited is a little more complex than we have, thus far, suggested. Consider the following further data, from the same accent:

(15) [ɹɒʊlʌ] roller   [ɹʌʊlənd] Roland
      [hɒʊli] holey   [hʌʊli] holy

What is the phonological status of the diphthong in *roller*? On the one hand, we have said that the [ɒʊ] allophone appears before a tautosyllabic /l/. On the other hand, it would appear that Maximal Onset would have us syllabify the /l/ into the onset position of the second syllable. But if the /l/ is indeed in that position, then we ought to get the [ʌʊ] allophone. Why, then, do we *not* get that allophone? Let us consider two possible responses.

One response is to say that speakers of this accent originally had a straightforward phonological rule, of the sort we have given, for the realization of the /ʌʊ/ phoneme, but that, as the accent has evolved, a **phonemic split** has emerged: the two vowels were in complementary distribution, but have come to occur in overlapping, parallel distribution. Evidence which is cited in support of this view is the emergence of minimal pairs, such as *holey* vs *holy*. Here, it is argued, we have clear evidence that a phonemic split has occurred.

We might make the following objection to the analysis just cited: it is failing to take note of an important generalization concerning the members of minimal pairs such as *holy* and *holey*, namely that those containing the [ʌʊ] vowel consist of only one morpheme (they are morphologically *simple*), whereas those containing [ɒʊ] consist of more than one morpheme (they are morphologically *complex*). Furthermore, in each case, the relevant vowel occurs before an /l/ which, in the morphologically complex cases, is morpheme-final.

One way of expressing this sensitivity of the phonological rule to morphological structure is to say that the rule applies *prior* to the affixation of the suffix in cases like *holey*, as follows:

(16)   root: /hʌʊl/

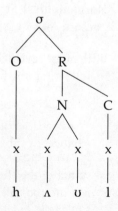

(17) Application of /ʌʊ/ rule

/ʌʊ/ → [ʊʊ] before tautosyllabic /l/

(18) Affixation

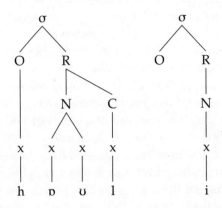

(19) Resyllabification

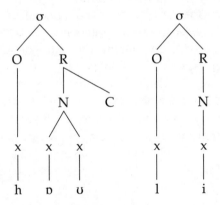

This analysis requires appeal to a further notion: that of **resyl-labification**. The idea is that, while the /l/ is *initially* syllabified into coda position, it is *re*syllabified, after affixation, and according to the Maximal Onset principle, into the empty onset in the suffix (the idea of resyllabification into an empty onset position being part of the motivation for postulating empty onsets).

There is an important point to be made with respect to cases such as this. It is that there may be cases where a phonetic distinction acts as the basis for minimal pairs (in this case, pairs like *holy/holey*) where, none the less, we do not wish to postulate a phonemic distinction between the two segments. In such cases, the members of those pairs will almost always differ in their morphological structure (in this case, *holy* is morphologically simple, while *holey* is morphologically complex), and that difference will affect the application of generalizations which govern the allophones of phonemes.

Notice that, in the case of many non-London accents, the reverse ordering of phonological generalizations and resyllabification applies in the case of the generalizations which yield the [i:] and [i:ə] allophones of the /i:/ phoneme and the clear and dark allophones of the /l/ phoneme. We saw that, in many accents, in words like *peel* and *feel*, the allophone of /i:/ is [i:ə], and the /l/ allophone is [ɫ], as in [fi:əɫ] (*feel*). In cases like *feeling*, the /l/ is resyllabified into the empty onset of the suffix -ɪŋ, thus: [fi:lɪŋ]. We want to say that the rule (as defined on p. 80) which governs the allophones of the /l/ phoneme, and the rule which governs the allophones of the /i:/ phoneme, apply *after* resyllabification.

We will take the view that, while the phonemic principle, in distinguishing between contrastive and non-contrastive distinctions, embodies an important insight into the nature of phonological organization, its conception of phonological contrast is at times overly restrictive, since it is defined without reference to the influence of morphological and syntactic factors on phonological organization. We will therefore, at times, allow our analyses to, as it were, override the phonemic principle. In doing so, we are not abandoning the notions which find a place in that principle; rather, we are allowing that morphological factors may influence phonological processes.

7.8 Summing Up

We have adopted here an account of the syllable as a phonological constituent. We have said that the sub-parts of syllables have differing degrees of perceptual salience, so that the nucleus is more salient than the other parts of the syllable. This is perhaps why, in many languages, coda consonants so often diminish in degree of stricture, to the point of 'fading away' altogether. This is what has happened to the realizations of the /ɹ/ phoneme in many accents of English, for instance: at one stage in their history, /ɹ/ was realized in coda position. It is also what happened to many case endings (suffixes which consisted of a vowel and one or more coda consonants) in the history of English nouns (English nouns used to have case endings such as -um, -am, -ans, -uns, all of which have disappeared over time).

The loss of case endings in English nouns involved another factor, however: not only are nuclei more salient perceptually than coda consonants, but, in languages like English, some nuclei in a word (*stressed* nuclei) are more salient than others. It is to the subject of word stress in English that we now turn.

Exercises

1   For each of the following words, say how it is syllabified, and why alternative syllabifications are disallowed (e.g. the word /kwɒntɪti/ (*quantity*) is syllabified as /kwɒn.tɪ.ti/; the syllabification /kwɒ.ntɪ.ti/ violates English phonotactics, since /nt/ is not a permissible branching onset; the syllabification /kwɒnt.ɹ.ti/ is ruled out by the principle of Maximal Onset):

    (a) /ɹəvaɪz/   (*revise*)   (b) /pɹədɪkʃən/ (*prediction*)
    (c) /ɹɛzɪdɛnʃəl/ (*residential*) (d) /ɛmpəɹə/   (*emperor*)
    (e) /dʒæpəniːz/ (*Japanese*) (f) /kɒndʌkt/   (*conduct*)

2   Of the following monosyllabic phonological representations, say which are English, and which are non-English, representations for monosyllabic words. For each non-English form, say why it is not possible:

    (a) /pnɪt/   (b) /psɪt/   (c) /pɹɒt/
    (d) /plɛt/   (e) /pɪh/   (f) /ɹpæt/

3   Examine the following data from the Cockney variety of London English:

(a)	[lɔɪʔ]	'light'	(b)	[laɪdi]	'lady'
(c)	[fiːlɪn]	'feeling'	(d)	[fiːw]	'feel'
(e)	[gɜːw]	'girl'	(f)	[bɒʔu]	'bottle' (bisyllabic)
(g)	[fɪlʌ]	'filler'	(h)	[fiːwʔʌ]	'filter'
(i)	[waɪ]	'way'	(j)	[weɪʔ]	'wet'

The sound [w] may be a realization of the /w/ phoneme, as in (i) and (j). However, it may also be an allophone of the /l/ phoneme, as in (d), (e) and (h). In (f), /l/ becomes a syllabic '[w]', namely [u]. That is, there is phonemic overlapping between /l/ and /w/. In which contexts does the [w] allophone of /l/ occur? Your answer should be expressed in terms of syllable structure.

4 Further transcription practice

Transcribe, with as much detail as possible, the following words as you would utter them in everyday casual speech, indicating syllable boundaries (with a full stop) and any syllabic consonants (e.g. *battle*: [bæ.ʔl̩], for some speakers):

hunting   kettle   derived   university   wrecking   suppose   divine serene   perhaps

8

English Word Stress

8.1 Introduction: Is English Word Stress Predictable?

We have already noted that the native speaker's perceptual capacities allow her or him to say how many syllables a word has, in the absence of any conscious knowledge of what a syllable might be, or how it might be defined. Similarly, English speakers can tell which syllable in a word receives most stress, in the absence of any conscious knowledge of exactly what 'stress' might be. While the native speaker may not know consciously what stress is, it seems clear that, the more stressed a syllable is, the more salient it is, perceptually. For instance, most native speakers of English will agree that, in the word *photography*, it is the second of the four syllables which is most stressed, that, in *kangaroo*, it is the last of its three syllables which receives most stress, and so on. It is equally striking that the native speaker can judge that, while the final syllable in *kangaroo* receives more stress than either of the others, the first syllable in turn receives more stress than the second. The first, third and fourth syllables of *photography* are **unstressed** and are less salient than the second syllable. The second syllable of *kangaroo* is unstressed and is the least salient syllable in that word. Let us say that the syllable in a word which receives most stress has **primary stress**, and that syllables such as the first syllable in *kangaroo* have **secondary stress**; while syllables which have neither primary nor secondary stress are unstressed syllables. We could therefore say that a given word will have a kind of *stress pattern*: in the case of *kangaroo*, a syllable with secondary stress, followed by an unstressed syllable, followed by a syllable with primary stress. We can informally represent primary stress by placing a superscript diacritic (^{1}) immediately before the start of the appropriate syllable, and secondary stress by using the superscript diacritic (^{2}), leaving any unstressed syllables without a diacritic, thus: [^{2}kæŋgə^{1}ɹuː].

It seems clear that knowledge of the stress patterns of words does not require instruction, and children acquiring their native language are not normally given explicit instruction by their parents as to where the stresses in a word are placed. Having established that, let us consider the following question: how does the speaker know what the stress pattern of a given word is? It seems reasonable to suggest that the speaker simply has to *memorize* the stress pattern of each word as it is learned. After all, for any given word, the speaker has to memorize the sequence of phonemes which (partly) make up the phonological form of the word. The speaker may just as well memorize the stress pattern while he or she is at it. One might object that this means that an average speaker has a vast number of stress patterns to memorize (as many stress patterns as there are words in her vocabulary), but we know that human beings are very good at storing large amounts of information of this sort in memory. Again, we can point to the vast number of phonological forms which the speaker clearly must have in mental storage; it is, surely, not too tasking to an organism which has that kind of storage capacity to store the stress patterns of those words along with the sequence of phonemes which partly make up their phonological form.

But this is not to say that there are no unconsciously stored generalizations governing stress patterns, just as there are generalizations concerning allophonic realizations and syllable structure.

We know that, for some languages, such as Modern Greek, the stress pattern of a word is entirely arbitrary; there appear to be no generalizations concerning word stress patterns. We also know that some languages have fixed stress: the stress always falls on a given syllable (in French, for instance, it always falls on the final syllable of the word). Let us consider some evidence in favour of the idea that the native speaker of English has internalized generalizations concerning word stress patterns in English. Take the following three sets of trisyllabic English nouns:

(1) elephant   potato   kangaroo
     cinema   horizon   ballyhoo

You will agree that the words in the first column have primary stress on the first syllable, those in the second column on the second syllable, and those in the third column on the third syllable. Given that the words do not differ as to syntactic category (they are all nouns) and do not differ in terms of total number of syllables, it looks as though there is no generalization concerning word stress in English trisyllabic nouns. Consider, however, the following *non-English* trisyllabic nouns:

(2) Gigondas   Zaventem   tavola

The first of these words is French (it is the name of a town, and a wine, in the Southern Rhône Valley), and is stressed, like all French words, on the final syllable. The second is Dutch (it is the name of a town in Flanders, and the name of Brussels airport); it is stressed, in Dutch, on the first syllable. The third is the Italian word for 'table' and is stressed, in Italian, on the first syllable.

What is striking about English speakers who know no French, Dutch or Italian, and have never heard the words before, is that they show a very strong tendency, on first encountering them, to mispronounce these words by stressing them on the *second* syllable, as follows: [ʤɪˈgɒndəs], [zəˈvɛntəm], [təˈvoʊlə]. If the English speaker has no word stress generalizations, this tendency is deeply puzzling, since that would mean that given a word one has never encountered before (especially a foreign word), one should display no tendency to prefer placing the stress on any particular syllable. One might expect a given individual to utter each word variably on different occasions, with each of the three possible stress patterns. And even if a given speaker alighted, arbitrarily, on a given stress pattern and stuck to it thereafter, one would expect variation from speaker to speaker. But this does not happen: the pronunciation in which the second syllable is stressed is the one which English speakers tend to opt for. You will probably agree, especially if you know any French, Dutch or Italian and have heard English speakers mispronouncing words in those languages, that this kind of pronunciation is 'typically English'.

But *what* is 'typically English' about it? We can only answer that question if there are word stress generalizations, and if we know what they are. We will now look at the form those generalizations might take.

8.2   Word Stress Assignment, Syntactic Category and Syllable Structure

Stress assignment in English is sensitive to the syntactic category of the word. Firstly, words of a non-lexical category (such as pronouns, conjunctions, articles, as opposed to nouns, verbs, adjectives and adverbs), often referred to as function words, are not normally stressed. Secondly, stress assignment differs between nouns on the one hand and verbs and adjectives on the other. In the vast majority of cases, primary stress in English nouns does not fall on the final syllable. We will look at those cases first. We may divide them into two sets: those where the stress falls on the second-last (penultimate) syllable (as in (3a) below) and those where the stress falls on the third from the last (the antepenultimate) syllable (as in (3b) below):

(3a)	potato	(3b)	camera
	apartment		cinema
	relation		quantity
	prediction		emperor
	disaster		custody

We have argued that there must be some means of predicting where stress falls in such cases. We have already mentioned the notion of syllable *weight*: we said that, if a syllable branches anywhere within its rhyme, then it is a *heavy* syllable, whereas syllables with non-branching rhymes are *light* syllables. There is one important exception to this generalization: a syllable which has schwa ([ə]) as its sole nucleus vowel is light, even if it branches. That is, a syllable with a sole schwa followed by one or more coda consonants counts as a light syllable. For instance, in the adjective *personal*, the last syllable is [nəɫ] for many speakers, and therefore counts as a light syllable.

Another way of putting this is to say that a syllable with schwa as its sole nucleus vowel is by definition an unstressed syllable.

It is the distinction between light and heavy syllables which governs stress assignment in these cases: if the penultimate syllable is heavy, it is stressed; otherwise it is the antepenultimate syllable which is stressed. The forms in (3a) all have heavy penultimate syllables, i.e. a penultimate syllable which contains a long vowel, as in *apartment*, or a diphthong, as in *relation*, or a short vowel plus a coda consonant, as in *prediction*.

It is this generalization which underlies the English speaker's marked tendency to place the stress on the second syllable in the three words in (2). There are exceptions to this generalization, which perhaps explains why it is only a tendency (albeit a very strong one) to stress words such as those in (2) on the second syllable. Words such as *confetti*, which has a light penultimate syllable, and thus should have stress on the antepenult, are none the less stressed on the penult.

Let us now turn to nouns where the stress falls on the final syllable. Some examples are given in (4):

(4) canal   lament   degree   July   ravine   estate
     marzipan Bucharest ballyhoo   fricassee magazine balloon

These nouns all have something in common: the last syllable is heavy. It consists of either a short vowel and one or more coda consonants (as in *canal* and *lament*) or a long vowel (as in *degree*) or a diphthong (as in *July*) or a long vowel/diphthong and one or more coda consonants (as in *ravine* and *estate*). This is true for all nouns in English with stress on the final syllable. Note, however, that while it is true to say that all nouns with stress on the final syllable have heavy final syllables, it is not true to say that all nouns with final heavy syllables have stress on that syllable. One of the striking facts about the class of English nouns with stress on the final syllable is that it is a very small class, and that many of the words in it are loanwords which are not terribly common, and many speakers may pronounce them with stress on a non-final syllable (as in *marzipan, fricassee, ballyhoo, magazine, Bucharest*, for many speakers). This class, then, is very much a class of exceptions.

Verbs and adjectives in English are quite different from nouns in that there are many of them with final stress, as in (5) and (6):

(5)   Final-stressed verbs

deny   revise   concede   produce   correct   reply

(6)   Final-stressed adjectives

divine   obscene   serene   alive   correct   immune

It is clear from these examples that, where a verb or adjective has final stress, the final syllable is heavy. The fact that verbs readily allow stress on the final syllable whereas nouns do not can be seen in verb/noun pairs such as *con¹tract* vs *¹contract*, *di¹gest* vs *¹digest*, *pro¹duce* vs *¹produce*, etc., where the verb takes final stress but the noun does not.

We have identified two factors which play a part in word stress assignment in English: the syntactic category of the word (nouns behave differently from verbs and adjectives) and syllable weight. We are now in a position to offer a full explanation for the marked tendency, shown by English speakers, to stress the foreign words in (2) on the penultimate syllable: the speaker knows (even if unconsciously) that the word is a noun (perhaps because it is, say, self-evidently a place name, or is used to refer to an object) and the syllable-weight generalization comes (unconsciously) into play, resulting in a stressing on the penultimate syllable, which is heavy.[1] As we have seen, there are exceptions to English stress assignment rules, but that is not to say that there are no rules (generalizations) at all.

Let us now consider some further factors which may affect word stress assignment in English.

8.3   Word Stress Assignment and Morphological Structure

We have already considered the relationship between syllable structure, morphological structure and phonological generalizations. We saw that when suffixes are added to a root, that can have the effect of changing syllabification, which can in turn have the effect of influencing the realization of the phonemes in the word which results from the addition of the suffix(es). The addition of suffixes can also have consequences for the way that a word is stressed.

Suffixes may be subdivided into **inflectional** and **derivational** suffixes. The addition of an inflectional suffix is often said to produce 'a different form' of the word one would have if the suffix had not been added. For instance, when the suffix -*ing* is added to the verb *obscure*, the resulting word, *obscuring*, is said to be a form of that verb; when the plural suffix is added to the noun *tractor*, the resulting word *tractors* is a form of that noun, etc. But when a derivational suffix is added to a word, it is said to produce, not a different form of the same word, but another word. Thus, when the suffix -*ly* is added to an adjective, say *bold*, the result, the adverb *boldly*, is a distinct word. Similarly, when the suffix -*ness* is added to an adjective, as in *boldness*, the result is a distinct word. Other examples of derivational suffixes in English are -*ity* (as in *personal/personality*), -*ee* (as in *divorce/divorcee*), -*al* (as in *person/personal*), -*ian* (as in *Wagner/Wagnerian*), -*ic* (as in *atom/atomic*), etc.

It has often been observed that some English derivational suffixes, when added to a word, have the effect of shifting the stress, while other suffixes, both inflectional and derivational, do not have this effect. Notice that, of the derivational suffixes we have listed, -*ity*, -*ee*, -*ian* and -*ic* all have this effect, but none of the others do. These two classes of suffix are referred to as the **stress-shifting** and **stress-neutral** suffixes, respectively, and one of the striking facts about the stress-neutral suffixes is that, even where their addition would result in making a syllable heavy, and thus stressable, it remains unstressed. For instance, the verb *bully*, because its final syllable is not heavy, is stressed on the preceding syllable. But if we add the third person singular suffix, the resulting form of the verb (*bullies*) does indeed have a heavy final syllable; none the less, that syllable remains unstressed: it is as if stress, assigned on the basis of syllable weight and syntactic category, has already been fixed, and affixation of this category of suffix cannot change it. And yet, with some derivational suffixes, addition of the suffix does indeed shift the stress, quite independently of syllable structure. For instance, the third syllable of *personal* is heavy yet unstressed (the suffix -*al* does not shift the stress in *person*), while the third syllable of *personality* is light (the /l/ has been resyllabified into the onset of the next

English Word Stress

3 Further transcription practice

Transcribe, with as much phonetic detail as possible, the following words as you would utter them in everyday casual speech, indicating syllable boundaries, and primary and (where applicable) secondary stress:

commandment entity margarine export (noun) export (verb) scrutineer audacity

9

The Rhythm *of* English

9.1 The Foot

We have said that the syllable is a phonological constituent which is closely connected to the perception of the speech signal: in the perception of speech, the nucleus, the obligatory part of a syllable, is the most salient part of a syllable. Similarly, stressed syllables are perceptually more salient than unstressed syllables.

Recall that we distinguished between (a) unstressed syllables, (b) syllables which have secondary stress, and (c) those which have primary stress. We said that, in the word *kangaroo*, for instance, the first syllable has secondary stress, the second is unstressed and the third has primary stress. We represented primary and secondary stress as follows: [²kæŋgə¹ɹuː].

Either of these conventions will suffice if we confine our interest to the level of the word. But they will not suffice if we wish to represent the way levels of stress and relative perceptual salience operate when words are combined into phrases. Take the phrase *kangaroo court*, for instance. The single syllable of the word *court* has more stress than any of the syllables in *kangaroo*, and that is not easy to represent using either of the methods just mentioned. Additionally, when *kangaroo* appears in the phrase *kangaroo court*, the secondary and primary stresses appear to switch round.

It is those kinds of stress pattern, beyond the level of the word in isolation, and the rhythm of English speech, that we will be concerned with in this chapter. We will now postulate a phonological constituent which, we will claim, figures in our perception of the speech signal and is a central part of the rhythm of English speech: **the foot.**

Let us say that a syllable which receives primary or secondary stress is the obligatory part of a foot, and that a foot in English consists of a stressed syllable (whether primary or secondary stressed) and any unstressed syllables which intervene between it and the following stressed syllable. According to this view, the word *witty* contains a single foot, consisting of a stressed syllable followed by a single unstressed syllable. Similarly, the word *cinema* contains a single foot, which consists of a stressed syllable followed by *two* unstressed syllables. Monosyllabic words, such as *hit*, contain a foot which consists only of a stressed syllable.

We represented syllable structure in terms of branching tree structures. Many phonologists also represent foot structure in terms of branching trees. We will represent any syllable which has either primary or secondary stress with an 'S', indicating that it is strong with respect to weak unstressed syllables, which we label with a 'W'. A stressed syllable and any unstressed syllables with which it forms a foot may then be represented as follows:

(1)[1]

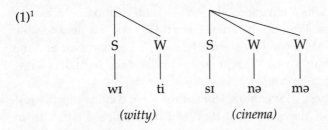

S	W	S	W	W
wɪ	ti	sɪ	nə	mə

(witty)   (cinema)

The bottom-most level of representation in this diagram is the level of the syllable. At that level, the S labels represent strong (stressed) syllables and the W labels represent unstressed syllables. It is important to bear in mind that stress levels are *relational*: rather than a stressed syllable being definable in absolute terms, one syllable is more or less stressed *in relation to another*.

The next level of representation up from the syllable (the lines above the S and W labels in this diagram) is that of the foot. Each word in (1) consists of a single foot, the first word consisting of a binary-branching foot and the second word consisting of a tertiary (three-way)-branching foot.

Monosyllabic *lexical* words contain, by definition, a single stressed syllable. We will take it that they contain a single, *non-branching* foot. We will therefore represent such words as having a single S-labelled syllable (indicating that it is stressed), dominated by a non-branching foot node, thus:

(2)

(hit)

This diagram represents two claims. The first is that the syllable in question is stressed (labelled S). The second is that, because it is stressed, it constitutes a foot which happens not to have a branching structure, since there are no unstressed syllables following it.

Monosyllabic non-lexical *function* words, such as pronouns (e.g. *he, she, me, it*), prepositions (e.g. *in, on, at*), articles (*a, an, the*) and conjunctions (e.g. *and, but, if*) are typically unstressed. We will therefore represent them with a W-labelled syllable, but no foot structure above that level (since a foot by definition must contain a stressed syllable), thus:

(3)

(it)

The relational nature of stress levels can be seen clearly in words which have both a primary stressed syllable and a secondary stressed syllable, such as *photograph*. It is clear that the first syllable in this word has more stress than the second (it is strong with respect to the second). It is equally clear that the third syllable has more stress than the second, and that the first syllable has more stress than the third. That is, the first syllable has primary stress, the second is unstressed, and the third has secondary stress. We may therefore represent the foot structure of the word as consisting of two feet, the first of which is stronger than the second, as follows:[2]

(4)

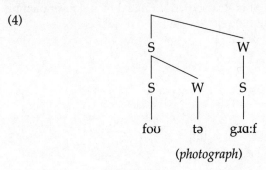

(*photograph*)

Note that the S/W notation is used to represent the relative strength *both* of syllables within a foot *and* of sequences of feet: the S/W notation shows that the first syllable is strong with respect to the second, and also shows, at a higher level, that the first *foot* is strong with respect to the second.

In words such as *colonnade* and *kangaroo*, on the other hand, it is the second of the two feet which is the stronger, since it has a secondary stressed syllable followed by an unstressed syllable followed by a primary stressed syllable:

(5)

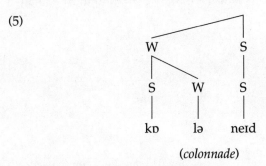

(*colonnade*)

Words such as *champagne*, which have a primary stressed and a secondary stressed syllable, but no unstressed syllables, contain two feet, each of which contains only a strong syllable. However, one of those feet is strong with respect to the other, thus:

(6)

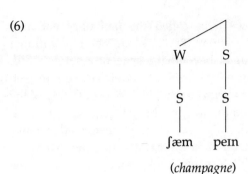

(*champagne*)

In this word, the second of the two feet is the stronger, whereas, in a word such as the noun *export*, it is the first of the two feet which is the stronger:

(7)

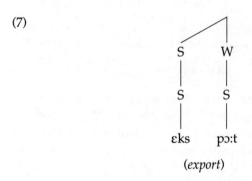

(*export*)

Recall that monosyllabic function words are typically unstressed (and are thus simply labelled with a W). Monosyllabic words of a lexical category may form branching feet with such words, as in the phrase *hit it*. Thus a phrase such as *hit it* contains exactly the same foot structure as a single word such as *witty*:

(8)

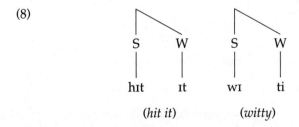

(*hit it*)   (*witty*)

Thus, the constituent we have called the foot does not map directly onto the word: there may be more than one foot within a word, and a foot may extend beyond the span of a single word. Furthermore, a word may not be exhaustively divisible into feet. For example, words such as *America* contain a foot consisting of the stressed second syllable and the two unstressed syllables which follow it; the first, unstressed, syllable, is a 'stray' unstressed syllable, which is part of the word, but is not integrated into the foot structure formed by the three syllables which follow it (rather in the same way that an /s/ preceding an onset consonant may be part of a word without being integrated into syllable structure):

(9)

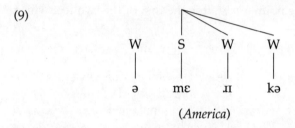

(*America*)

The first, 'stray' unstressed syllable here is parallel to the monosyllabic function words discussed above: at the level of the word, it is not integrated into foot structure. In this way of analysing English foot structure, words which begin with one or more unstressed syllables, such as *America, about* and *maroon*, do not consist of a single foot which begins with a W syllable. Since we are denying that there are W-S feet in English, it is only at the level of larger units such as the phrase that such unstressed syllables may be integrated into foot structure, as in the verb phrase *saw America*:

(10)

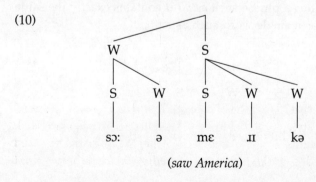

(*saw America*)

We saw that words like *champagne* and *export* are bisyllabic and contain two feet. These are fundamentally different from words such as *maroon*, which are also bisyllabic but begin with a 'stray' unstressed syllable and contain only one foot, which consists of the stressed syllable:

(11)

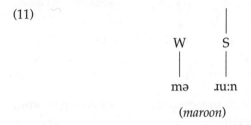

(maroon)

9.2 Phonological Generalizations and Foot Structure

One of the reasons for postulating the foot as a phonological constituent is that, just as some phonological generalizations are sensitive to syllable structure, so some phonological generalizations are sensitive to foot structure. Take the generalization, or rule, of **Flapping**, in many dialects of American English. Under this generalization, /t/ and /d/ are realized as an alveolar tap (also known as a flap) between vowels, as in *Betty* and *bedding* ([bɛɾi] and [bɛɾɪŋ]). But the rule does not apply if a foot boundary occurs adjacent to the /t/ or /d/. Thus, the generalization does not cover cases such as *attacker*, or *a tacker*, since, in those cases, a foot boundary intervenes between the first vowel and the /t/, thus:

(12)

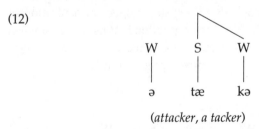

(attacker, a tacker)

If a foot consists, as we have said, in a stressed vowel followed by any immediately following unstressed syllables, then a word such as *attacker* contains a single foot (which begins with the stressed syllable) preceded by a 'stray' unstressed syllable, as in the first syllable of *America*. Thus the first syllable is not a part of the foot in which the /t/ appears, whereas in a word such as *Betty*, it is:

(13)

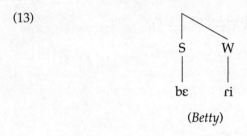

(*Betty*)

Note that Flapping also occurs in feet which are formed across word boundaries, as in *hit it* ([hɪɾɪt]):

(14)

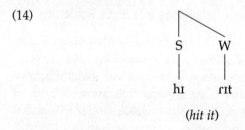

(*hit it*)

That is, Flapping is not sensitive to word boundaries or to the morphological structure; rather, it is foot structure which matters in the application of Flapping: Flapping only applies *foot-internally*.

Another example of a generalization which is often said to be sensitive to foot structure is the rule of Aspiration. We have already noted that we must acknowledge that there are degrees of aspiration of voiceless stops in English. However, aspiration is at its strongest when the voiceless stop in question is in foot-initial position, as in *party* and *appearance*, whose foot structures are given in (15):

(15)

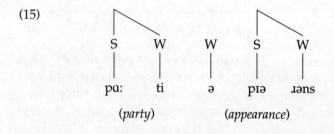

(*party*)   (*appearance*)

Aspiration applies foot-initially (although there may be some degree of aspiration in other positions).

9.3 The Rhythm of English: Stress Timing and Eurhythmy

It is often said that the rhythm of English is **stress-timed**. What this means is that the regular recurring beats found in the speech of English speakers (the rhythm of English speech) fall on stressed syllables. That is, stressed syllables in English occur at more or less equal intervals. Languages like English are often said to be distinct from languages like French in this respect in that, in languages like French, each syllable is said to occur at a more or less equal interval (languages of that sort are often, therefore, said to be *syllable-timed*).

One of the consequences of this kind of rhythm is that English feet may consist of a stressed syllable followed by a sequence of unstressed syllables, as in the phrase *heard in the park*, in which the stressed syllable in *heard* is followed by two unstressed syllables, or the phrase *heard it in the park*, where *heard* is followed by three, or the phrase *heard it in the announcement*, where it is followed by four.

Having said that English allows for really quite extensive sequences of unstressed syllables, it has to be said that the 'ideal' or optimal rhythmic structure is one in which strong and weak syllables alternate, in an S-W-S-W pattern. It appears to be the case that such sequences of 'alternating opposites' are optimal in a perceptual sense: they seem to make the speech signal more easily decoded. Such optimal rhythmic structures are often referred to as **eurhythmic** structures. It follows from this that the optimal, most eurhythmic, foot structure is a simple S-W structure, with only one unstressed syllable to the right of the stressed syllable. Foot structures with more than one W syllable are therefore less eurhythmic, less optimal, than those with only one, and the greater the number of unstressed syllables, the less eurhythmic or optimal the foot.

This preference for eurhythmy extends to sequences of feet: sequences of S and W feet are also more eurhythmic than other sequences. For instance, in the sentence *I want a cup of coffee*, there is an S-W-S sequence of three feet in the verb phrase, each of which is itself an S-W sequence of syllables; it is eurhythmic both at the level of sequences of syllables and at the level of sequences of feet:

(16)

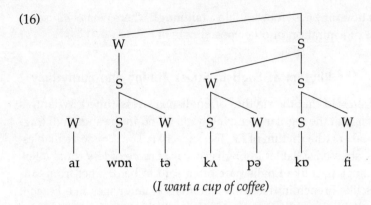

(*I want a cup of coffee*)

However, in many cases, a given combination of words may potentially create a phrase which is less than eurhythmic, and indeed may potentially result in adjacent S-labelled feet. This results from the fact that, in English phrases, it is the final word which is most stressed, as in the phrase *black bird*, discussed earlier. This **phrasal stress** rule seems to hold for most types of phrase in English, as in *slowly ate* (verb phrase), *very yellow* (adjective phrase), *into London* (prepositional phrase), and *very slowly* (adverb phrase). It also seems to apply at the level of the sentence, as we can see from the example just given in (16): the predicate verb phrase is more salient than the preceding subject noun phrase. Where the phrasal stress rule brings about adjacent S-labelled feet, it appears that 'evasive action' can be taken. Let us consider some examples.

Take the words *academic, Tennessee* and *champagne*. Clearly, *academic* has primary stress on the third syllable and secondary stress on the first syllable; the other syllables are unstressed. The foot structure of the word is as follows:

(17)

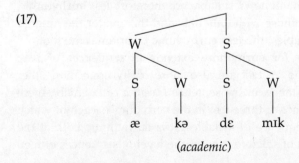

(*academic*)

Tennessee also contains two feet, the second stronger than the first. However, the second foot consists simply of a stressed syllable, with no unstressed syllables following it:

(18)

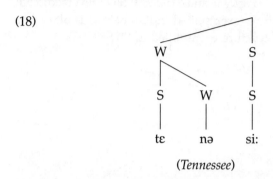

(*Tennessee*)

Champagne also has two feet, as we have already seen, the first of which consists of a syllable with secondary stress and the second of which consists of a syllable with primary stress:

(19)

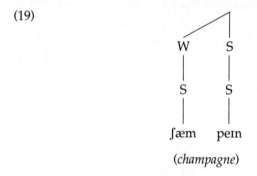

(*champagne*)

In each of these three cases, the word consists of two feet, the second of which is strong with respect to the first. However, when these words appear in phrases where the strongest of the two feet is immediately followed by the stressed syllable of another foot, and where that syllable must be more heavily stressed than the preceding one, a kind of 'stress clash' results, in which, rather than a eurhythmic sequence of S and W feet, an S-S sequence of feet occurs. In situations such as this, a rule of **rhythm reversal** applies. Consider some such phrases, e.g. *academic banter, champagne breakfast, Tennessee*

Williams. Note that, in each case, the rule for phrasal stress assignment means that the second of the two words must have greater stress than the first. Note too that the primary and secondary stresses in the words *academic, champagne* and *Tennessee* have reversed. That is, the offending structure (exemplified in (20) below) is altered to the more eurhythmic structure exemplified in (21).

(20)

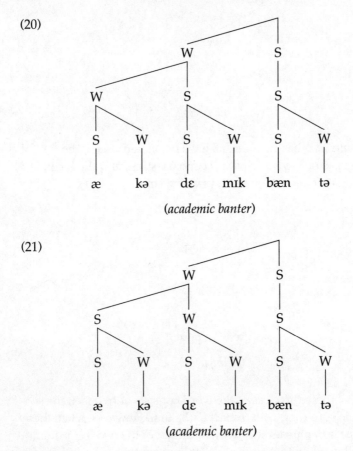

(*academic banter*)

(21)

(*academic banter*)

This process of rhythm reversal is quite regular in English. Other examples are easily found; consider *Piccadilly* vs *Piccadilly Circus, Heathrow* vs *Heathrow Airport, Dundee* vs *Dundee marmalade, thirty-four* vs *thirty-four books, good-looking* vs *good-looking tutor,* and so on. As we have seen, in English phrases, it is the head, rather than a preceding modifier, which bears the most stress. Rhythm reversal occurs whenever a word containing a weak-strong sequence of feet is combined, to form a phrase, with a word whose first syllable is the first syllable of a foot (i.e. is stressed). That is, rhythm reversal operates, within the context of phrases, on feet, not syllables, reversing weak-strong sequences of feet, rather than weak-strong sequences of syllables. Another way of putting this is to say that the reversal process reverses a sequence of a secondary stressed syllable and a primary stressed syllable when it is followed by a primary stressed syllable within a phrase.

Reversal does *not* operate on a sequence consisting of an unstressed syllable and the first syllable of a foot, as in *maroon sweater*. The word *maroon* contains a single foot, which consists only of a stressed syllable with no following unstressed syllables; that foot is preceded by a 'stray' unstressed syllable (just like the unstressed syllable in *America*, shown in (9) above), thus:

(22)

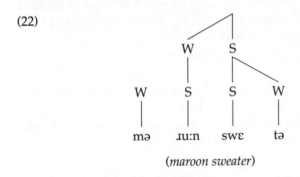

(*maroon sweater*)

While *maroon sweater* contains an S-S sequence of *syllables*, it does *not* contain an S-S sequence of *feet*, and it does not therefore undergo rhythm reversal. The pervasive effects of the rhythm reversal rule are said to constitute evidence for the existence of the foot as a constituent in the phonology of English. Furthermore, the fact that words like *maroon* do not undergo reversal can be taken as evidence for our claims (a) that English feet always begin with a stressed syllable, and (b) that English words are not necessarily exhaustively divisible into feet. In other words, a word like *maroon* is *not* to be analysed as consisting of a foot with a W-S sequence of syllables.

The claim that rhythm reversal operates at the level of sequences of feet, rather than at the level of sequences of syllables, is supported by the fact that it operates in phrases such as *good-looking tutor*, which, prior to reversal, has the following structure:

(23)

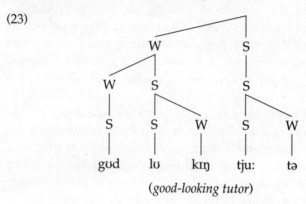

(*good-looking tutor*)

If reversal operated at the level of sequences of S and W syllables (rather than feet), it would not affect the sequence *looking* and *tutor*, which has an alternating S-W-S-W structure. It is at the level of the foot that the S-W sequencing is violated.

The most striking aspect of reversal is that it demonstrates the interaction of syntax and phonology. The conditions under which reversal operates are partly determined by a syntactic fact about English: the fact that modifiers typically precede heads in English phrases. This, combined with the fact that it is the head which receives more stress than the modifier, brings about the reversal phenomenon.

Reversal also interacts with morphological structure: it operates within words which contain a suffix which itself takes stress. Take the verb *condemn*. It consists of two feet, the second stronger than the first:

(24)

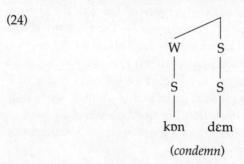

(*condemn*)

The suffix -*ation* is one of those English suffixes which takes stress. It consists of a single binary branching foot, and when it is added to *condemn*, the resulting word *condemnation* consists of three feet in a W-S-S sequence:

(25)

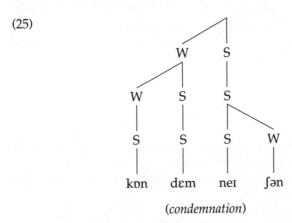

(*condemnation*)

This structure meets the conditions for reversal, which then applies to yield the S-W-S sequence of feet in *condemnation*.

It is true, of course, that one can, in fact, utter phrases such as *academic banter* with primary stress on the third syllable of *academic*. When one does this, one is usually contrasting some aspect of the phrase with some other possibility. One might be stressing, for instance, that one means *academic* banter and not some other kind of banter, such as *adolescent* banter. The most important fact about this phenomenon, often referred to as **contrastive stress**, is that it is a *discourse phenomenon*: one could not make sense of such a stressing if it were not accompanied by an appropriate discourse setting in which one's interlocutor stands a chance of understanding what other possibilities one is contrasting the rhythm-reversed adjective *academic* with. The following exchange is an example:

(26) A: I do enjoy academic banter, you know. (rhythm reversal)
B: What kind of banter?
A: [2]Aca[1]demic banter. (contrastive stress; no rhythm reversal)

The stress pattern here is none the less distinct from that given in (20) above, since the stressed syllable of *banter* is less stressed than the primary stressed syllable of *academic*. What examples such as these suggest is that reversal is a metrical phenomenon which interacts with morphology and syntax, and can be described *independently of discourse context*, whereas contrastive stress is a phenomenon which *cannot* be described independently of discourse context. This suggests that it is possible, and perhaps necessary, to distinguish those phenomena which can be analysed independently of context of utterance from those which cannot.

Notes

1   The metrical trees we present here are abbreviated, for reasons of lack of space. Because metrical structure is determined by syllable structure, we ought, strictly speaking, to show metrical trees built upon syllable structure trees, as follows:

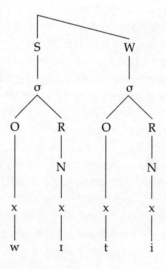

The trees used in this chapter do not actually show that it is the structure of the rhyme, and not the entire syllable, which is crucial in determining metrical structure. However, they will suffice for our purposes.

2   We label the non-branching foot with an S, consistent with our treatment of monosyllabic words of a lexical category.

Exercises

1 Draw metrical trees for each of the following words. Begin by drawing the foot structure. Where a word contains more than one foot, draw a superordinate S/W or W/S branching structure, showing which of the two feet is strongest:

(a) pretty   (b) collided   (c) sentiment
(d) bat   (e) nightingale   (f) kangaroo
(g) rabbi   (h) contract

2 Draw metrical trees for the following phrases. Show the tree for (d) both before and after rhythm reversal has applied:

(a) sacked a worker
(b) delighted agents
(c) very pretty
(d) Piccadilly Circus

10

Connected Speech *and* Intonation

10.1   Reduction, Lenition, Assimilation and Elision

We have said that English is stress-timed, and that the number of unstressed syllables intervening between two stressed syllables may be quite high. Given that it is possible to have many such intervening unstressed syllables, and that the stressed syllables ought to be more or less equally spaced, this puts pressure on such intervening syllables to simplify in various ways. In this section, we will consider the following sorts of simplification: vowel reduction, consonant assimilation, consonant lenition, and, finally, the elision (non-pronunciation) of consonants and vowels.

By **vowel reduction**, we mean a reduction in the length of a vowel, usually accompanied by a change in its quality. Vowel reduction in unstressed syllables is extremely common in English. Take the word *robust*. The first syllable of that word, being unstressed, is very often pronounced with a short [o], rather than the full diphthong [oʊ], and may even be pronounced simply with a schwa. Such reductions, particularly reduction to schwa, are even more likely if the first syllable forms part of a sequence of unstressed syllables, as in *heard it in the robust speech*. The most common form of vowel reduction is reduction to schwa, which, of all vowels, requires the smallest deviation of the tongue body from the neutral position and requires no lip rounding; it is also the shortest of all the vowels. It seems to make phonetic sense to say that vowels should reduce to schwa in unstressed syllables, particularly if the syllable in question is one of a series of such syllables. Clearly, the larger the number of phonetic segments the speaker must articulate in the more or less fixed amount of time between stressed syllables, the more pressing it is that those segments require as little articulation as possible: reduction in length and in deviation from the neutral position both save articulatory time.

A reduction in the amount of articulation required is also at work in the second of these phenomena, **consonant assimilation**. Take the phrase *fat thing*, for instance. This is often pronounced as [fæt̪θɪŋ], with a dental stop at the end of the word *fat*. The alveolar stop in this word has shifted its place of articulation in anticipation of the following dental sound; that is, it has assimilated to the following sound in terms of place of articulation. Similarly, the phrase *fat cat* may (depending on one's accent) be articulated as [fækkæt], and the phrase *fat man* as [fæpmæn]. We have already seen examples of this kind of assimilation within words, but it occurs across word boundaries in connected speech too.

We have also seen cases within words where nasal stops assimilate in place of articulation to a following consonant; this happens regularly across word boundaries as well. The phrase *ten pin bowling* is often pronounced as [tʰɛmpʰɪmboʊlɪŋ], in which the alveolar nasals in *ten* and *pin* assimilate in place of articulation to the following bilabial stops. Similarly, in the phrase *ten kinds*, often pronounced as [tʰɛŋkʰaɪnz], the alveolar nasal in *ten* assimilates to the following stop and becomes velar.

Another common sort of assimilation in place of articulation occurs when a [s] or a [z] occurs at the end of one word and is followed by an [i] or a [j] at the beginning of the next, as in the phrase *miss you*. In cases like this, it is very common for the alveolar fricative to assimilate partially to the following palatal sound, and become palato-alveolar, as in [mɪʃu]. A similar kind of assimilation occurs when a [t] or [d] at the end of one word is followed by an [i] or [j] at the beginning of the next, as in *hit you*, often pronounced [hɪʧu]. In this case, the alveolar stop [t] and the palatal approximant [j] have, as it were, 'coalesced' into a palato-alveolar affricate. This kind of coalescence therefore entails assimilation both for place of articulation and for manner of articulation.

By **consonant lenition**, we mean a diminution in the degree of constriction of a consonant and/or the voicing of a voiced consonant, and/or the length of time the constriction is held. An example is the process of Flapping in American English, in which /t/ and /d/ are realized as [ɾ], a voiced alveolar flap (or tap) between a stressed and an unstressed vowel, as in *bedding* and *betting*: [bɛɾɪŋ]. Since the voiced alveolar flap is like a short [d], the flap requires a shorter closure than either /t/ or /d/, and thus constitutes a saving in articulatory time. The voicing of /t/ to [ɾ] constitutes a kind of assimilation, and thus an articulatory saving: the stop is assimilated in voicing to the surrounding vowels.

A common type of consonantal lenition is the reduction of oral stops to glottal stop, as in *put it right* when pronounced as [pʊʔɪʔɹaɪʔ]. Since glottal stops require no oral articulation, the tongue is free, during the articulation of the glottal stop, to assume its position for the following segment, and this means a saving in articulatory time and effort. In many varieties of English, reduction of voiceless stops to glottal stop is common in coda position, particularly in unstressed syllables, as in sentences such as *I didn't know that she'd gone*, where the function word *that* is frequently pronounced as [ðəʔ], especially if the following word begins with a consonant. Accents of English vary considerably with respect to the range of sites where reduction is possible, and with respect to the range of stops which are subject to reduction (/t/ generally seems to be more widely subject to reduction than /p/ or /k/).

The most extreme form of lenition is complete elision of segments (which is already evident in the phrase *ten kinds*, discussed above). This happens with both consonants and vowels. Take the phrase *the sixth month*: in isolation, *sixth* would be [sɪksθ], but the dental fricative tends not to be pronounced at all in the phrase *the sixth month*, which is typically pronounced as [ðəsɪksmʌnθ]. Where clusters of consonants arise through the combination of words into phrases, they are frequently reduced in this way. An example is the phrase *crisp bowl*, often pronounced as [kʰɹɪsboʊɫ], with the final stop in *crisp* elided. Elision of consonants is also common in words of a non-lexical category, as we have already seen. Words such as *and*, *have* and *of* are often pronounced with elided consonants, as in *Bill and Ivy* ([bɪlənaɪvi]), *should have gone* ([ʃudəgɒn]), *cup of tea* ([kʰʌpətʰiː]).

Vowel elision may result in the loss of an entire syllable, as in *university* when it is pronounced as [juːnɪvɜːsti]. This is clearly of some considerable help in reducing the number of unstressed syllables to be articulated. Alternatively, elision of a vowel may result in the syllabification of a consonant, as in *support* when it is pronounced [s̩pɔːt], or in the pronunciation of *and* as [n], as in *Bill and Ivy*, pronounced as above.

These connected speech phenomena are all much more widespread in a language like English, in which codas and onsets may contain consonant clusters, and in which quite large sequences of unstressed syllables may intervene between stressed syllables; it is noticeable that English speakers are prone to carry over these reduction and elision phenomena into their speech when they speak languages like Spanish and Italian, which have a different rhythm, and tend not to allow for reduction of vowels to schwa. For instance, the Italian verb *parlare* (to speak) should be uttered [perˈlɛre], without schwas, but a typical English learner error is to pronounce it as [pəɹˈlɑːɹe], with the vowel in the first syllable, which precedes the stressed syllable, reduced to schwa. It seems clear that such phenomena are intimately connected with the rhythm of English.

10.2 Insertion of [ɹ]

Recall that we have distinguished between rhotic and non-rhotic accents of English: non-rhotic accents do not allow /ɹ/ in rhymes, so that words such as *car*, when uttered in isolation, do not contain an [ɹ], whereas in rhotic accents, they do. A distinction is often made between 'linking [ɹ]' and 'intrusive [ɹ]' in (mainly) non-rhotic accents of English. Put simply, linking [ɹ] is the [ɹ] which is said to occur between the two words of phrases like *far away*, and intrusive [ɹ] is said to occur between the two words of phrases like *saw America*. It is widely agreed that, in the former case, there was an 'r' sound at the end of the first word at some stage in the history of the language; in the latter case there never was. In order to understand the status of the [ɹ] which occurs in cases such as these, we need to consider how we analyse non-rhotic accents of English, which is where the phenomenon has arisen. But there is more than one way of analysing the phonological status of non-rhotic accents; we will have to consider the alternatives. Let us begin by comparing some RP and SSE (Scottish Standard English) words:

(1)   [ɹ] in RP and SSE

	RP	*SSE*	
(a)	[ɹiːm]	[ɹim]	ream
(b)	[ɹæt]	[ɹɛt]	rat
(c)	[pʰɹɒd]	[pʰɹɔd]	prod
(d)	[bɹɪk]	[bɹɪk]	brick
(e)	[nɪə]	[niːɹ]	near
(f)	[ɛə]	[eːɹ]	air
(g)	[mɔː]	[mʉːɹ]	moor
(h)	[mɔː]	[moːɹ]	more
(i)	[kʰɑː]	[kʰɐɹ]	car
(j)	[pʰɜːd]	[pʰʌɹd]	purred
(k)	[vɜːʤ]	[vɛɹʤ]	verge
(l)	[bɜːd]	[bʌɹd]	bird
(m)	[kʰɑːd]	[kʰɐɹd]	card

It is clear that SSE has [ɹ] in places where RP does not. We might say that there are two such places: before a consonant (as in (j)–(m)) and word-finally (as in (e)–(i)). However, both accents have [ɹ] word-initially (as in (a) and (b)) and after a consonant (as in (c) and (d)). A simpler way of expressing the distribution of [ɹ] in these accents is, as we have seen, to refer to syllable structure: in RP, [ɹ] may appear in onsets (as in (a)–(d)), but not in codas (as in (e)–(l)), whereas, in SSE, [ɹ] may appear in both onsets *and* codas. It is important to bear in mind that the term 'rhotic' in this context does not refer to the *kind* of 'r' *articulations* found in rhotic accents, such as the alveolar trill [r] or the tap [ɾ], as opposed to the approximant [ɹ]. As can be seen from the data above, the two accents are *not* differentiated with respect to the kind of 'r' articulation they have. And even if SSE consistently had, say, [r] rather than [ɹ], that kind of fact is not what the term 'rhotic' (as used here) refers to. Rather, it refers to the presence of *some* kind of 'r' articulation (*any* kind) in rhymes.

It is one thing to say that rhoticity and non-rhoticity are phonological properties of accents. But what is the nature of that phonological distinction? We have assumed that it is a difference in phonotactics: in rhotic accents, the /ɹ/ phoneme may appear in rhymes, whereas in non-rhotic accents, it may not. But this is far from being the only analysis. Let us try to argue for the position we have adopted. It is clear enough that in the SSE data above, the phoneme /ɹ/ is present in the phonological form of each of the root morphemes present, as in /ɹim/ (*ream*), /keɹ/ (*car*) and /keɹd/ (*card*). So, in a rhotic accent, the *phonological* segment /ɹ/ may appear in both onsets and codas. But what of non-rhotic accents? All we have established thus far is that the *phonetic* segment [ɹ] has a distribution in rhotic accents which differs from its distribution in non-rhotic accents.

Let us consider two hypotheses. Under the first (the one we have adopted; let us call it hypothesis A for the moment), we claim that the phoneme /ɹ/ may not appear in rhymes in the phonological form of morphemes (thus the difference between the accents is a difference in phonotactics). This is plausible enough; recall that languages have many arbitrary, language-specific, phonotactic constraints of this sort. For instance, in English, /ŋ/ may not appear in onsets, and /h/ may not appear in rhymes (while /hoʊld/ (*hold*) and /bəhaɪnd/ *behind* are well-formed, /aɪh/ is not, for instance). These are simply arbitrary facts about English; other languages impose no such constraints (most dialects of Arabic, for instance, allow /h/ in rhymes, and many languages allow /ŋ/ in onsets). So, under hypothesis A, /ɹ/, like /h/, may not appear in rhymes. This means that the phonological forms of the root morphemes in (e)–(m) above do not contain an /ɹ/. The morphemes 'air' and 'card', for instance, are, in non-rhotic accents, /ɛə/ and /kɑːd/ respectively, under this analysis. Consider, however, the following data from a non-rhotic accent (RP):

(2) (a) [hɪə] hear   [hɪəɹɪŋ] hearing
   (b) [ɛə] air   [ɛəɹɪŋ] airy
   (c) [mʊə] moor   [mʊəɹɪŋ] mooring

(d)	[pɔː]	pour	[pɔːɹɪŋ]	pouring
(e)	[bɑː]	bar	[bɑːɹɪŋ]	barring
(f)	[pɜː]	purr	[pɜːɹɪŋ]	purring

The appearance of [ɹ] in these cases ('linking r'), does not falsify hypothesis A. We can maintain that hypothesis by continuing to insist that the root morphemes in question lack /ɹ/ and that, when a suffix which begins with a vowel is added to a root which ends in a vowel, an [ɹ] must be *inserted* in the realization of the word in question. Let us refer to this version of hypothesis A as 'the Insertion Hypothesis'. It is not unreasonable: we could say that this generalization is one of the phonological generalizations in the non-rhotic speaker's unconscious linguistic knowledge. However, the following data show that, expressed that way, the generalization cannot be correct:

(3)	(a)	[siː]	see	[siːɪŋ]	seeing
	(b)	[duː]	do	[duːɪŋ]	doing
	(c)	[seɪ]	say	[seɪɪŋ]	saying
	(d)	[laɪ]	lie	[laɪɪŋ]	lying
	(e)	[tɔɪ]	toy	[tɔɪɪŋ]	toying
	(f)	[noʊ]	know	[noʊɪŋ]	knowing
	(g)	[baʊ]	bow	[baʊɪŋ]	bowing

Clearly, it is not true that an [ɹ] must be inserted when a root ending in a vowel (*any* vowel) is followed by a suffix beginning in a vowel. One can, however, amend the Insertion Hypothesis by claiming that a root ending phonetically in one of the vowels from the set [ə], [ɑː], [ɔː] and [ɜː] (not just any vowel) must have an [ɹ] added when it is followed by a suffix, or another word, which begins with a vowel. This version certainly saves the Insertion Hypothesis. (Note that words ending in the diphthongs [ɪə], [ɪə] and [ɛə] count as words ending in schwa ([ə]), under this formulation.)

Note that the root-final vowels in (3) are either [iː] or [uː], or one of the diphthongs, such as [aɪ] or [aʊ], which end in a high vowel articulation. This set of vowels have something in common: they are *high* vowels. The adherent of the Insertion Hypothesis can argue that insertion takes place only after *non-high* vowels. Thus, of the long vowels, insertion will not take place with either [iː] or [uː]. Of the diphthongs, those ending in a high vowel articulation will not trigger insertion. None of the short vowels ([ɪ], [ɛ], [æ], [ʌ], [ʊ] and [ɒ]) occurs root-finally, so they could never trigger insertion.[1] We can claim that the phonological changes in the history of such accents were sensitive to the height of the preceding vowel. In doing so, the adherent of the Insertion Hypothesis can therefore claim to be formulating the relevant phonological rule in terms of a **natural class** (the non-high vowels, as opposed to the high vowels). By 'natural class' is meant a set of sounds, or phonemes, which have a clear phonetic common denominator which defines that class to the exclusion of all other sounds, or phonemes, in a language. For instance, the set {/b/, /d/, /g/} in English constitutes a natural class (the class of voiced stop phonemes in English), whereas the set of English consonant phonemes {/h/, /ŋ/, /b/} does *not* constitute a natural class. Similarly, the set of RP vowels appealed to here, {/iː/, /ɪ/, /uː/, /ʊ/}, constitutes the set of high vowels in RP, whereas a set such as {/iː/, /ʌ/, /ɔː/} does not constitute a natural class (the three vowels share no common denominator which would allow us to pick out that set alone from the set of RP vowel phonemes). Phonological rules, and historical phonological changes, when they apply to a set of sounds or phonemes (rather than to a single sound or phoneme), tend to apply to natural classes. Analyses which appeal to natural classes are therefore preferred over those which appeal to *ad hoc*, arbitrary sets of sounds or phonemes.

So the Insertion Hypothesis is plausible. But one might argue that, in place of it, we should argue for a different approach, one version of which we will call 'the Deletion Hypothesis'. Under this hypothesis, we would say that the morphemes in question have an /ɹ/ in their phonological representation. The generalization is not that /ɹ/ is forbidden from codas in the phonological representation of morphemes in non-rhotic accents. Rather, the generalization is that /ɹ/ is *not realized* (alternatively, *is deleted*) in coda position. Under this analysis, *air*, *card*, etc. have the phonological form /ɛəɹ/, /kɑːɹd/, etc. When *air* has the suffix *-y* added, the /ɹ/ undergoes resyllabification into the empty onset position of the suffix. The derivation would look like this:

(4) root: /ɛəɹ/

Syllabification:

(5) Suffixation and resyllabification:

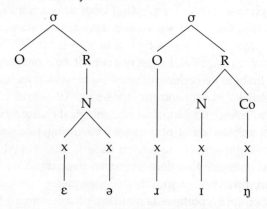

Under this way of looking at non-rhotic accents, the /ɹ/ can only be realized if there is an empty onset slot to 'rescue' it and, since the /ɹ/ in words like *card* is never in a position to get into such a slot (the *following* consonant does that), it *never* comes to be realized.

How are we to choose between these hypotheses? Each gets the phonetic facts presented (thus far) correct, but they are, apparently, distinct explanations of those facts. The Insertion Hypothesis offers a generalization based (quite crucially, as we will see) on sequences of *phonetic* segments, whereas the generalization expressed by the Deletion Hypothesis is sensitive to *phonological* sequences (/ɹ/ followed by a filled vs an empty onset). The reality of the matter, the generalization which the non-rhotic speaker has stored in his or her mind, is not available for inspection. We can base our choice only on evidence and argumentation. But the evidence given thus far equally supports both hypotheses.

There is some further evidence, however, which appears to support the Insertion Hypothesis over the Deletion Hypothesis. In many non-rhotic accents, [ɹ] appears after one of the postulated set of non-high vowels (namely, schwa) when the following word or suffix begins with a vowel, even though the word in question did not have an /ɹ/ historically. Examples are phrases such as: *Linda Anderson*, pronounced as [lɪndəɹændəsən], *law and order* ([lɔːɹənɔːdə]), and *draw a conclusion*, again pronounced with an [ɹ]: [dɹɔːɹəkənkʰluːʒən]. The phenomenon appears not to be restricted to a few stock phrases, but to be very general in many accents, if socially frowned upon in some circles. Speech communities vary as to whether this phenomenon ('intrusive r') occurs word-internally, as in *drawing*, pronounced as [dɹɔːɹɪŋ], as well as occurring between words, or only between words.

The adherent of the Deletion Hypothesis can respond to this phenomenon by postulating an /ɹ/ in the phonological form of these words, parallel to that found in the cases of 'linking r', so that *draw*, for instance, has the phonological form /dɹɔːɹ/. The final /ɹ/ will be realized only when there is an empty onset following, as in the case of 'linking r'.

Fortunately, there is further evidence from 'intrusive r' phenomena which supports one hypothesis over the other. As we have seen, the speech of speakers of most accents of English exhibits the phenomenon of vowel reduction, under which vowels are 'reduced' to a schwa pronunciation when they are unstressed. Word-internal examples are pairs like *photograph* and *photography*. As we have seen, the first vowel in *photograph* is the most stressed vowel in that word, and is not a schwa. In RP it would be [oʊ]. However, in the related word *photography*, the stress has shifted to the second syllable, with the result that the first syllable is unstressed and is pronounced as a schwa: [fətʰɒgɹəfi]. In cases such as this, many phonologists would say that the vowel in the first syllable is /oʊ/ in phonological representation, and that this is realized as schwa when unstressed.

Consider cases where this phenomenon happens at the end of a word. Take the word *piano*. In many accents, this is pronounced

confident that they can perceive different sorts of intonation, and they know that people can convey a variety of things by means of intonation. But what is intonation, in phonetic terms? The answer is that what we perceive as intonation is produced by a variety of phonetic means, the most important of which is **pitch**. By 'pitch' is meant rate of vibration of the vocal cords. We know what vocal cord vibration is. It is, put simply, the number of times per second that the vocal cords open and close: the faster the rate, the higher the pitch. We know that some individuals have a generally higher rate of vocal cord vibration than others: their pitch range is higher than that of others. We also know that, typically, women have a higher vocal cord vibration rate than men; that is, they typically have higher-pitched voices than men. But there are also immense variations, from one individual to another, in the normal pitch range of their speech.

In many cases, these variations are simply 'filtered out' in speech perception. We can tell whether a sound is voiced or not quite independently of what the rate of vibration is; simple presence or absence of vocal cord vibration will suffice as a perceptual clue (although there is more to it than that: English speakers can tell, from contextual cues, that a sound is 'phonologically voiced' even if, in a particular context, it has little or no vocal cord vibration).

We can change the pitch level at certain points during the course of an utterance. This can result in **pitch contours** at those points, so that the pitch can go from a given pitch to a higher one, thus producing a *rising pitch*, or **rise**. Equally, the pitch can go from a given level to a lower level, thus resulting in a falling pitch or **fall**. More complex still, the pitch can rise and then fall, resulting in a **rise-fall** contour, or it can fall and then rise, resulting in a **fall-rise** contour. Or the pitch level can remain more or less constant at the relevant point, resulting in a **level** tone.

In many languages, pitch differences play a role parallel to those played by other phonetic differences: they can act as the basis for minimal pairs. This is the case in the many tone languages of the world, in which a particular level of pitch, relative to another, or a particular pitch contour, can distinguish one word from another. For instance, in the Thai language, the phonetic sequence [na:] means 'aunt' when uttered with a high tone (a relatively high pitch). But it means 'face' when uttered with a falling tone. In these cases, we want to say that pitch differences are contrastive.

Distinctions such as 'high pitch' vs 'low pitch' are relative notions, in just the same way as the distinction between 'long vowels' and 'short vowels' is relative, and in the same way as the distinction between primary stressed vs secondary stressed vs unstressed syllables is relative, or in the same way as the distinction between strong and weak feet is relative. It is all very much a matter of perceptual distinctions between one kind of acoustic event and another.

Speakers of English do not exploit pitch differences in the way that speakers of tone languages do, but they do none the less exploit them, and it is those sorts of exploitation that are referred to as intonational phenomena. For instance, when speakers of many accents of English ask yes/no questions such as 'Are you going to the shops?', there is typically a rising pitch (a rise contour) on the last stressed syllable of the utterance (in this case, *shops*). We will transcribe a rising pitch by means of the symbol '↗' placed before the relevant syllable: 'Are you going to the ↗ shops?'. On the other hand, in a statement, such as 'John is going to the shops', the pitch tends to fall on the last stressed syllable. We will transcribe a fall with the symbol '↘' placed before the relevant syllable, as in 'John is going to the ↘ shops.' Accents vary with respect to the intonation of statements; there are accents, such as the Ulster one spoken in Northern Ireland, in which a rising pitch typically occurs in such utterances. We will briefly examine two further pitch contours below, and we will look at further functions of intonation, but first we must identify which parts of an utterance these intonation contours are superimposed on.

10.4 Tone Groups

In the speech of most speakers of English, there are typically stretches of one or more syllables in which the pitch contour (or tone) occurs. Those stretches are often referred to as **tone groups** (also called 'intonation groups' or 'tone units'). Within these groups, there is usually one particular syllable on which the tone occurs (mostly the last one), and this is referred to as the **tonic syllable** (also called 'the nucleus' or 'the intonation centre'). Tonic syllables are perceptually more salient than the other syllables within the tone group. Let us take an example. In 'Has he ↗ gone?', uttered with a rising pitch on the last syllable, we would want to say that the three syllables in question constitute a tone group and that the last syllable is the tonic syllable: it carries the rising pitch. In '↘ Tell me, has he ↗ gone?', uttered with a falling pitch on 'tell' and a rising pitch on 'gone', we would want to say that there are two tone groups, the first of which consists of the first two syllables and the last of which consists of the last three syllables. In the first tone group, the first syllable is the tonic syllable. In a given tone group, the tonic syllable must carry one of the tones we have cited above. We will mark the boundary between tone groups by means of a '/' symbol placed before the first syllable of the relevant tone group, as in '↘ Tell me / has he ↗ gone?'.

You will have noticed that the two tone groups in this case may be separated by a pause. You may also have noticed, if you have studied English syntax, that the tone groups in this case correspond to the major syntactic constituents of the utterance, namely (in this case) the two clauses in question. Sometimes the major syntactic constituents are phrases, as in 'For me, with a pregnant wife, life is rather hard.' In this case, there are tonic syllables on 'me', 'wife' and 'hard', and the tone groups correspond to two prepositional phrases and a clause. You may also have noticed that it is possible to utter the examples given here in other ways, with other syllables selected as the tonic syllable. We will return to that fact below.

10.5 The Functions of Intonation

It is common to distinguish different functions of intonation. One of these is its **attitudinal function**. This has to do with conveying more than is actually conveyed by the meanings of the words used. It is true that one can express one's attitude to what has been said explicitly by simply uttering some appropriate words. For instance, in response to the question 'Did you know that Mary was pregnant?', one might reply 'Yes, and, quite frankly, it surprises me.' One can convey attitudes in a variety of other ways, including the use of facial expressions and 'body language'. Some of these means involve the use of intonation. For instance, if a yes/no question such as 'Did you know that Mary was pregnant?' is answered '↘ yes', with a falling tone, the impression conveyed is one of certainty and finality. But if the same question is answered with the word '↗ yes' uttered with a rising tone, no impression of finality is conveyed. Rather, the impression given is that the person answering the question wants the questioner to continue in some way. These sorts of function of intonation can be manipulated by the speaker; if, for instance, one wants to attempt to shut off any further discussion of a subject, a clear falling tone can be used to convey that desire.

A **rise-fall** tone often conveys a sense of strong agreement or disagreement. We will transcribe this pitch contour using the symbols '↗ ↘' placed before the relevant syllable. For instance, given the query 'You're not having an affair with Mary, are you?', a reply '↗ ↘ No!', with a rise-fall would convey a strong denial, stronger than that conveyed by the same word uttered with a simple falling tone. Similarly, the statement 'Isn't Mary lovely!', when replied to with the statement '↗ ↘ Yes', uttered with a rise-fall would express strong agreement, stronger than that conveyed by the response '↘ Yes', uttered with a falling tone.

A **fall-rise** tone, transcribed with a '↘ ↗' before the appropriate syllable, often conveys a sense of 'agreement up to a point' or hesitant agreement. For instance, the response '↘ ↗ yes', to the statement 'Isn't Mary lovely?', suggests that the speaker has reservations.

Although we do not normally speak in a monotone, without significant pitch variation, one may do so, and thus convey boredom or a sense that what is being said is routine and uninteresting. This is what one often experiences when dealing with someone who has to perform the same verbal task many times, for instance when one is checking in for a flight at an airport and dealing with someone who is clearly bored by having to ask the same sequence of questions many times over.

Intonation may also have a **syntactic function**. A much-cited example is the use of intonation and pause to convey the difference between restrictive and non-restrictive relative clauses. Typically, non-restrictive relative clauses are represented in writing by the use of commas, as in 'The members of the government, who opposed sanctions, began to shout.' The corresponding sentence with a restrictive relative clause would be represented in writing as 'The members of the government who opposed sanctions began to shout.' The difference in the interpretation of the two is that, in the first case (the non-restrictive case), the suggestion is that all of the members of the government were in favour of sanctions, whereas, in the latter case (the restrictive case), not all of them were. In speech, the difference between the two can be represented by means of intonation. In the non-restrictive case, 'the members of the government' constitutes one tone group, and 'who opposed sanctions' constitutes another. In the restrictive case, 'the members of the government who opposed sanctions' constitutes a single tone group. The division between the two tone groups is signalled by means of the placement of a tonic syllable on the stressed syllables of 'government' and 'sanctions' and the presence of a pause between the two tone groups.

Notes

1 The short vowels [ɪ] and [ʊ], being high vowels, would fail to trigger insertion even if they did occur root-finally.
2 Given that the schwa uttered can be relatively long, there is little point in asking whether /ə/ or /ɜ:/ would be the right phonemes to postulate here, since the sound in question is not a realization of a phoneme. How long one prolongs the schwa sound depends on how long one hesitates; the purely phonetic notion 'vowel length' here bears only an indirect relation to the *phonological* notion of vowel length.

Exercises

1 Transcribe the following passage as you would say it in ordinary, everyday, casual speech. Transcribe any connected speech phenomena such as reduction, assimilation, syllabic consonants and elision:

She couldn't get the version she wanted. She'd asked a thousand times for a performance on an eighteenth-century violin. It made her angry with the shop manager and his staff. She saw a fat catalogue of record-ings available on CD, but they seemed unable to order any of them.

2 Read the following dialogue out loud. Mark any tone group boundaries. Mark pitch contours in front of the appropriate syllable. If you can imagine more than one pitch contour in a given tone group, transcribe the alternative pitch contour(s) and note the difference in conveyed meaning/speaker attitude:

A: Tell me, have you seen that film?
B: Yes! It was wonderful!
A: Did you go with John?
B: Yes, I did.
A: Was he interesting?
B: Yes, I suppose so.
A: Fascinating bloke.
B: Well, that's a matter of opinion.

11

Variation *in* English Accents

11.1 Introduction

In this chapter, we will consider some general aspects of accent variation. In the appendix which follows, a brief overview is given of five accents of English: General Australian English, London English, New York City English, Scottish Standard English (SSE) and Tyneside English, followed by an outline of the sorts of phenomena which give rise to divergence of accents over time.

Three of the accents we have referred to in this book (GA, RP and SSE) are viewed socially as 'standard' accents. The notion 'standard' is a social one: no linguist would claim that there is any coherent notion of inherent phonetic or phonological superiority, since such a notion simply does not make any phonetic or phonological sense. There can be no doubt that many people judge some accents to be superior to others, or take some accents to be standard accents and others to be non-standard accents. But those judgements are founded on non-linguistic factors, to do with social attitudes in the societies in question. From a strictly linguistic point of view, such judgements are, quite clearly, entirely arbitrary. For example, RP, the standard accent in England, is non-rhotic, and the non-rhoticity of RP is therefore judged by some (perhaps many) English people to be more prestigious than the rhotic accents found in many of the Western parts of England. But the standard accents SSE and GA are rhotic, and in the United States, it is the rhotic accents which are often judged to be more prestigious than the non-rhotic American accents (the judgement cannot arise in Scotland, where all native accents are rhotic).

Clearly, it is social attitudes which determine such judgements about accents, rather than the phonetic and phonological properties of the accents themselves. It is common to find social judgements to the effect that some accents are 'uglier' or 'harsher' than others. These judgements too are entirely arbitrary as far as phonetics and phonology are concerned. For instance, if the word *say*, pronounced as [saɪ] in London English, is judged 'ugly' by an RP speaker, then the RP speaker's own pronunciation of the word *sigh*, as [saɪ], ought also to strike the RP speaker as 'ugly'. Cases such as this show that it simply cannot be any phonetic properties of the sounds [saɪ] in and of themselves which induce the aesthetic judgement. Rather, such judgements also derive from and reflect social attitudes about what might, rather broadly, be called 'ways of life'. In Britain, most non-standard accents which are judged 'ugly' or 'uncivilized' are spoken in industrial or post-industrial urban areas; examples often cited are the working-class accents of London, Birmingham Liverpool, Belfast, Glasgow and Tyneside. Similar sorts of judgement are made in the United States, with respect to, for example, the broad New York City accent often referred to as 'the Brooklyn accent' (though it is not confined to the Brooklyn district of New York City).

Non-standard rural accents are, by contrast, often judged 'quaint', rather than 'ugly'; examples are accents from the Highlands of Scotland, from the West Country in England, or from the US Southern states. It is highly likely that these aesthetic judgements arise from the conscious or unconscious association of accents with the real or imagined ways of life of those who speak them. We will therefore stand back from such social attitudes and attempt to examine accent variation from the point of view of the phonetician and the phonologist.[1]

11.2 Systemic vs Realizational Differences between Accents

Let us begin by considering one of the differences between many accents in the North of England and many of those spoken in the South of England. In the latter accents, there is a phonological contrast between /ʊ/ and /ʌ/, which can be observed in pairs such as *book/buck, rook/ruck, put/putt*, and many others. That distinction is missing in many Northern English accents,[2] which have /ʊ/ in each member of the pair. That is, many Northern English accents simply lack the /ʌ/ phoneme, and thus the /ʊ/ vs /ʌ/ distinction: for them, pairs such as *put* and *putt* are homophones, not minimal pairs. We will refer to this sort of difference as a **systemic** difference[3] between two accents: the set of phonological contrasts (specifically, in this case, the vowel contrasts) of the speakers differ.

Systemic differences are widely attested. In many Scottish English and Scots accents, for instance, there is no equivalent of the /æ/ vs /ɑ:/ distinction, of the sort found in Southern English minimal pairs such as *ant/aunt, palm/Pam*, etc. In the Scottish English and Scots accents, each member of such pairs contains the same vowel phoneme, /ɐ/, which is realized as [ɐ]. Again, pairs which count as minimal pairs in non-Scottish accents are homophonous in Scottish accents. Similarly, as we have seen, while RP has a three-way distinction between /ɒ/, /ɑ:/ and /ɔ:/, GA has only a two-way distinction between /ɔ:/ and /ɑ/. This systemic difference means that there is a difference in the sets of words which are distinguished by means of these phonemes, as follows:

(1) | *Words of the type* | RP | GA |
|---|---|---|
| palm | /ɑ:/ | /ɑ/ |
| caught | /ɔ:/ | /ɔ:/ |
| cot | /ɒ/ | /ɑ/ |
| coffee | /ɒ/ | /ɔ:/ |

Systemic differences are not restricted to vowel systems. An example of a systemic difference in consonant systems is the contrast, found in many Scottish accents, between /ʍ/ and /w/, which is found in minimal pairs such as *whales* vs *Wales, whin* vs *win, what* vs *watt*, etc. That contrast is absent in most non-Scottish accents, which have a /w/ phoneme, but not a /ʍ/ phoneme. In those accents, the above pairs are homophones, rather than minimal pairs.

There are differences between accents which do not amount to a difference in the systems of phonological contrasts. Consider our discussion of dark and non-dark /l/ in chapter 7: we said there (7.6) that there is an allophonic rule in many accents of English, including GA and RP, to the effect that /l/ is realized as a velarized ('dark') lateral when it occurs in rhymes, but is realized as a non-velarized ('clear') lateral when it occurs in onsets. In many accents of the South of Scotland, in Australian English, and in some accents of the North of England, /l/ is realized as a dark lateral in all positions, so that /lʌl/ (*lull*), for instance, is realized as [ɫʌɫ], rather than [lʌɫ]. In Tyneside English, on the other hand, /l/ is consistently realized as a clear lateral in all positions, so that /lʌl/ (*lull*)[4] is realized as [lʌl].There is no question of postulating, in these sorts of case, a difference in the underlying system of contrasts: all three accents have /l/, but there is variation in the way that /l/ is realized. While there are languages in which the distinction between clear and dark laterals is contrastive, there can be no question of postulating such a phonological contrast in any of these accents of English: in the Southern Scottish and Australian cases, there are only dark laterals; in the Tyneside case, there are only clear laterals; and in RP and GA, while there are dark and non-dark laterals, the distinction is purely allophonic: the distinction lies at the level of realizations of a single phoneme. We will therefore refer to these sorts of difference as **realizational** differences.

Realizational differences involving vowels are very common. For instance, one of the differences between SSE and most non-Scottish accents is the presence of allophonic vowel length in SSE. This is absent in most non-Scottish accents, but this difference is a purely realizational matter. Take the contrast between /e/ and /o/ in SSE (as in *bait*, *boat*): that contrast is also present in most non-Scottish accents, including RP. In RP, the equivalent phonemes, /eɪ/ and /oʊ/, are, in all contexts, typically realized as [eɪ] and [oʊ] respectively. In SSE, however, /e/ is realized as either [e] (as in *bait*) or [e:] (as in *bare*), and /o/ is realized either as [o] (as in *boat*) or [o:] (as in *bore*), depending on the phonological context: the long realization occurs word-finally and before the voiced segments [ɹ], [z], [v], [ð] and [ʒ]; the short realization occurs elsewhere. Similarly, in GA, the /eɪ/ and /oʊ/ phonemes are realized as [e] and [o] before an [ɹ] which occurs in coda position, as in *pair* and *port*, but not in *pairing*.

Realizational differences can become systemic differences over time. For instance, at a stage in the history of RP when it was still a rhotic accent, the /i:/ phoneme was realized as [i:ə] before /ɹ/ in coda position, in much the same way as /iː/ is currently realized as [iːə] before /l/ in coda position. At that stage in the history of RP, pairs such as *feared/feed* and *beard/bead* differed in two respects: one had [ɹ], while the other did not, and one had [iː], while the other had [iːə]. With the gradual loss of the [ɹ] articulation in coda position, pairs like this became minimal pairs: [biːəd] (*beard*) vs [biːd] (*bead*). It is reasonable to say that, at that stage, a new /iːə/ phoneme (the ancestor of present-day /ɪə/) emerged. This process is known as a **phonemic split**: a distinction which was once allophonic becomes phonemic. In terms of differences between accents, we want to say that, at a point when both RP and, say, SSE were rhotic, they both had the /iː/ phoneme, but there was a realizational difference, in that RP, but not SSE, had an [iːə] allophone of the /iː/ phoneme. Now, however, there is a systemic difference: RP has an /iː/ vs /ɪə/ contrast which SSE lacks.

How can one tell, for a given difference, whether it is systemic or realizational? Let us examine a particular case, that of London English. By 'London English' (henceforth, LE), we do not mean the accent spoken by all natives of London; rather, we refer, albeit in a necessarily oversimplified way, to the speech of working-class natives of London.[5] It has been widely noted that speakers of LE typically utter words such as *lay, pay, say* with an [aɪ] diphthong, and we know that, in RP, these have an [eɪ] diphthong. Is this a systemic or a realizational difference?

The answer is that we cannot tell on the basis of this evidence alone. In order to establish whether there is a systemic difference between the accents, we must consider the system of contrasts in each accent. Specifically, we must ask: is there a phonetic [eɪ]/[aɪ] distinction in either accent, and if so, is it contrastive? We have already established that, in RP, there is such a distinction, and that it is contrastive (cf the minimal pairs *bay* vs *buy, Tay* vs *tie, say* vs *sigh*, etc.). What we must then establish is whether these pairs are also minimal pairs in LE: if they were to turn out to be homophones in LE, then we could, all things being equal, reasonably conclude that there is a systemic difference here, in just the same way that we concluded, on the basis of evidence from minimal pairs and homophones, that RP has an /ʊ/ vs /ʌ/ contrast, which many Northern English accents (with /ʊ/ alone) lack.

What we find is that these are indeed minimal pairs in LE: while *bay, Tay, say*, etc. have an [aɪ] diphthong in LE, *buy, tie, sigh*, etc. have an [ɔɪ] diphthong. In the absence of any further evidence to the contrary, we may conclude that there is no systemic difference here: the contrast which we found in RP is maintained in LE.

But the matter does not end there, since we also know that RP has a contrast between /aɪ/ and /ɔɪ/, as in *buy, tie, sigh* vs *boy, toy soy*. What we must now ask is whether this contrast is also sustained in LE, or whether these RP minimal pairs are homophones in LE. The answer is that the contrast is sustained in LE: while *buy, tie, sigh* etc. have [ɔɪ], *boy, toy, soy*, etc. have [oɪ].

We have now noted a related set of non-systemic (non-contrastive), purely realizational differences between RP and LE, which we might conceive of in terms of the articulatory and perceptual 'space' in which the realizations of a phoneme are located. We may depict this in terms of the vowel space diagram. Consider the phonetic realizations of the RP vowel phonemes /eɪ/, /aɪ/ and /ɔɪ/. Let us imagine that speakers of RP typically have diphthongal realizations of those phonemes whose starting points fall within the following sorts of articulatory 'zones' in the vowel space:

(2)

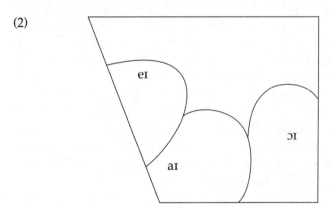

The speaker might well vary in her or his realizations of these phonemes. However, so long as the articulation of a particular vowel does not encroach upon the space of any of the others, *bay* will still be distinguishable from *buy*, and *buy* from *boy*. If, in the course of the historical development of the accent, the articulations of /eɪ/ and /aɪ/ were to become so close as to be perceptually indistinguishable, such that pairs like *bay* vs *buy* were both uttered as [baɪ], then the contrast would be lost. That phenomenon, which is widely attested in the histories of human languages, is referred to as a **phonemic merger**: where once a phonemic contrast was present, it came to be collapsed.[6] An example from American English concerns the contrast between /ɑ/ and /ɔ:/ which, as we have seen, is present in GA in pairs such as *cot*/*caught*. The contrast appears to have been merged for many speakers in certain parts of Pennsylvania, with *cot* and *caught* being homophones: [kʰɑt] (although there is variation in the precise realization of the merged vowel). The merger appears to have occurred in other parts of North America, including Canada, and parts of Utah and Nevada.

Clearly, no merger has occurred in the LE cases cited above: while the realization of /eɪ/ has indeed 'shifted' to [aɪ], the realization of /aɪ/ has, in turn, shifted, to [ɔɪ], and the contrast is thus maintained. Similarly, while the realization of /aɪ/ has shifted to [ɔɪ], the realization of /ɔɪ/ has in turn shifted, to [oɪ], and again the contrast has thus been maintained.[7] This kind of phenomenon, which is fairly widespread, is often referred to as a **vowel shift**. A parallel shift is evident in the variety of Australian English known as General Australian, where the /i:/ phoneme has diphthongized to [ɪi], thus encroaching, to some extent, on the space of /eɪ/. The /eɪ/ phoneme has in turn shifted to [ɐɪ], with a fairly low, central, unrounded starting point, thus encroaching on the perceptual space of /aɪ/. In turn, /aɪ/ has shifted to [ɒɪ], thus encroaching on the space of /ɔɪ/. However, the /ɔɪ/ phoneme appears not to have taken 'evasive action', so [ɒɪ] and [ɔɪ] are contrastive. The point to be borne in mind is that vowel shifts are purely realizational: they do not involve a change in the number of phonological contrasts.

We asked whether the realization of /aɪ/ as [ɔɪ] resulted in the destruction of a contrast which is present in RP. We might equally ask whether the realization of the /ɔɪ/ phoneme as [oɪ] in LE results in the destruction of a contrast found in RP; the answer is that, although RP speakers may well utter both [ɔɪ] and [oɪ], the phonetic difference between the two, while perceptible, is never contrastive: one cannot cite minimal pairs involving the two. So there is no phonemic contrast which would be collapsed by uttering /ɔɪ/

as [ɔɪ] (the RP speaker is free to do so, without risk of conflating a contrast). For the LE speaker, while the realization of /eɪ/ has encroached upon the 'space' of /aɪ/, and the realization of the latter has encroached upon the space of /ɔɪ/, the realization of the latter has not encroached upon the space of any other phoneme.

11.3 Perceptual and Articulatory Space

The simplest system of vowel phonemes[8] found in the world's languages is the three-vowel /i/, /u/, /a/ system, typically depicted within the vowel space as:

(3)

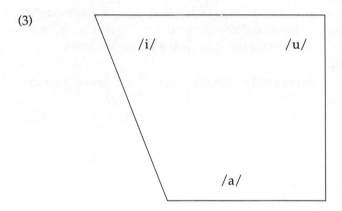

The realizations of the vowel phonemes in a system like this can vary considerably; it will matter little in terms of the hearer's identification of a given vowel phoneme if /i/ is realized as an [e]-type vowel, so long as it is relatively front, unrounded, and relatively high. Nor will it matter if /u/ is realized as an [o]-type vowel, so long as it is relatively high, relatively back, and rounded. Similarly, it will not matter whether realizations of /a/ are front (like [a]), back (like [ɑ]), or central (like [ɐ]), so long as they are relatively low and unrounded. That is, each vowel phoneme has quite a large perceptual and articulatory space.

A slightly larger vowel system, frequently encountered in the world's languages, has mid vowels:

(4)

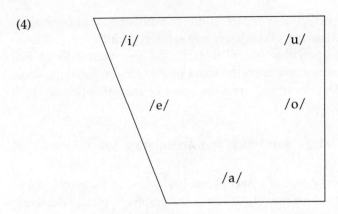

In a system like this, the vowel space is a little more crowded: it *will* matter whether a realization of /i/ is [e]-like, or if a realization of /u/ is [o]-like. But it will not matter if a realization of /e/ is [ɛ]-like, so long as it is not [a]-like. Nor will it matter if a realization of /o/ is [ɔ]-like.

In a slightly larger system, there are contrasts between high-mid and low-mid vowels:

(5)

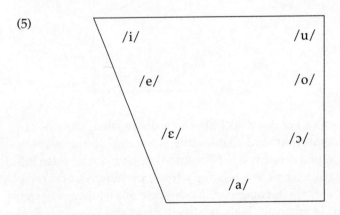

In this kind of system, there is even less articulatory and perceptual space for each vowel phoneme: it will matter if the realizations of /e/ are [ɛ]-like, for instance.

Many English accents have relatively large vowel phoneme systems, often containing, for instance, as many as three or four 'a'-type phonemes, as in RP's front /æ/, central /ʌ/ and back /ɑ:/. This

142

means that shifts in realization can easily result in one phoneme encroaching upon the space of another. And this notion of articulatory and perceptual 'space' has a bearing on the question of *which* pairs of vowel phonemes we should consider when attempting to establish whether a given vowel difference is systemic or not. One way of answering this question is to say that one should consider vowel phonemes which are in some sense 'adjacent' in articulatory and/or perceptual terms. This is what we did when we considered the [eɪ] vs [aɪ] distinction: they are adjacent in that the starting points of both diphthongs are front, non-high and unrounded. We might equally have considered the [ɛ] vs [eɪ] distinction, since [e], the starting point for the latter, is close to [ɛ] in articulatory terms. Indeed, one finds that the /ɛ/ phoneme is often realized as an [eɪ] diphthong in LE (thus, *well* can be pronounced as [weɪw]). This, however, does not cause merger of the /ɛ/ vs /eɪ/ contrast since, as we have seen, /eɪ/ is realized as [aɪ].

The main difficulty one encounters in considering adjacent vowel sounds is that a given vowel can be adjacent to many (perhaps most) of the other vowel sounds found in a particular accent. As we have just seen, [eɪ] is adjacent to both [aɪ] and [ɛ]. It is also adjacent to [ɜ:], since the starting point for [eɪ] is front, mid and unrounded, and [ɜ:] is central, mid and unrounded. As it happens, [ɜ:] has not shifted in LE, but it has in other accents. In the Liverpool accent, for instance, it has fronted to [ɛ:], so that *work* and *bird*, which are pronounced [wɜ:k] and [bɜ:d] in RP, are pronounced [wɛ:x] and [bɛ:d] in Liverpool. This means that the realization of /ɜ:/ has encroached upon the articulatory and perceptual space of the adjacent vowel phoneme /ɛ/. However, the phonemic distinction between /ɜ:/ and /ɛ/ is maintained in Liverpool, since the former is long with respect to the latter, as in *bird* vs *bed* ([bɛ:d] vs [bɛd]) and thus distinguishable from it. For many Tyneside speakers, /ɜ:/ has been retracted and rounded in some words, thus encroaching on the space of /ɔ:/. Thus *work* is pronounced [wɔ:k] by many speakers. This has resulted in a loss of the /ɜ:/ vs /ɔ:/ contrast in a particular set of words, so that pairs such as *walk/work* and *bird/bored* are homophones rather than minimal pairs.

It appears that vowel articulations are especially susceptible to this 'shifting around' phenomenon and it is because of this that the majority of differences between accents are differences in the articulation of vowels, rather than of consonants. This is perhaps because of the nature of vowel articulations, which all have a stricture of open approximation. Furthermore, the more open the vowel, the more open the approximation, and the less contact there is between the tongue and the other parts of the oral cavity. It seems clear that, for any given phonetic segment, we are unlikely to hit on exactly the same articulation each and every time we attempt it. Not every [d] we utter will have exactly the same part of the tongue closing against exactly the same part of the alveolar ridge for exactly the same length of time with exactly the same amount of vocal cord vibration beginning and ending at exactly the same time. So variation is inherent in speech.

But it appears to be even more inherent in vowel articulations than it is in, say, stops, since it is much harder to feel where one's tongue is in one's mouth when one produces a vowel than when one produces, say, a stop. One can feel the lips close together for the articulation of a bilabial stop, and one can feel the tongue against the alveolar ridge when one produces an alveolar stop, so that the articulatory difference between the two is easily discerned by the speaker. But when one produces, say an [e:] as opposed to an [ɛ], it is much harder to feel what one's tongue is doing. One can therefore easily 'overshoot' or 'undershoot' and end up with articulations which encroach upon the space of another, adjacent, vowel phoneme. Vowel articulations, in short, form a continuum; there are no abrupt, discrete divisions between them.

Parallel to this articulatory continuum, there is a perceptual one. Recall that our 'cardinal vowels' are merely reference points, based on an arbitrary carving up of the available vowel space and the available parameters of tongue height, frontness/backness, and roundedness, all of which are a matter of degree, rather than a matter of absolutes. Once an [e]-type sound begins to lower, at what point does it become an [ɛ]-type sound? Once an [æ]-type sound begins to raise, at what point does it become an [ɛ]-type sound? The answer is that it is impossible to say with any certainty. Little wonder, then, that when some American English speakers say *bad*, speakers of many accents of British English think that they are saying *bed*: their [æ]-type sound has raised to what is perceived as an [ɛ]-type sound.

The most important point is that our perception of acoustic events is heavily dependent on the mentally represented system of phonological contrasts which we have in our native accent. It is also vital that, for a phonemic distinction to exist, it must be based on a phonetic distinction which is perceptible to human beings. Those phonetic differences can be minute, but they must be perceivable. If a language does not have a large vowel phoneme inventory, the realizations of each vowel phoneme are much more 'free to roam' in the available articulatory and perceptual space.

There are consonantal continua too, but there is a little more in the way of discrete divisions among consonants than among vowels. A bilabial articulation, for example, is radically distinct from an alveolar one, since the tongue is not implicated at all in the former, and the lips need not be involved in the latter. But even then, we have seen, particularly among consonantal articulations which are more vowel-like, that a gradual transition from alveolar to labial is indeed possible, as we have seen with [w] realizations of /l/. Once a secondary velar articulation is present in the pronunciation of an alveolar lateral, it can become the primary articulation, the original alveolar stricture can be lost altogether, and a new bilabial stricture can emerge.

11.4   Differences in the Lexical Distribution of Phonemes

There is a further kind of variation between accents in which the phonological representation of words is concerned, but which is not systemic variation. For instance, in many accents of the North of England, there is some kind of /æ/ vs /ɑ:/ distinction, parallel to that found in RP. The actual vowel quality of the 'long a' often differs from that of RP. Many West Yorkshire speakers have a much more front articulation for 'long a' than RP speakers; very often the difference is between a short [a] and a long [a:], with the vowel qualities being the same, and the two vowels differentiated only with respect to length. None the less, the phonemic distinction is there, and functions as the basis of minimal pairs such as *ant/aunt* and *Sam/psalm*. We can say that West Yorkshire's /a/ vs

/a:/ distinction is parallel to, or equivalent to, RP's /æ/ vs /ɑ:/ distinction.

But speakers of such Northern English accents (and indeed of GA) often utter a short vowel in words which would be uttered with a long vowel by the RP speaker. Examples, for many Northern speakers, are *bath, class* and *glass.* What we want to say about this sort of difference is not that the Northern English speaker lacks the 'long a' vs 'short a' phonemic distinction (in the way that Scottish speakers do) but that the phonological form of those particular words contains the short, rather than the long, phoneme. We can illustrate this as follows:

(6) Systemic difference vs lexical distribution difference

	Phonemic *'long/short a'?*	*Phonological forms* *of ant, aunt, bath*
RP speaker:	Yes	/ænt/, /ɑ:nt/, /bɑ:θ/
Northern speaker:	Yes	/ant/, /a:nt/, /baθ/
Scottish speaker:	No	/ɛnt/, /ɛnt/, /bɐθ/

Such differences are very susceptible to variation between different accents in the range of words which have one phoneme rather than the other in their phonological representations. They are therefore less general in nature, and more idiosyncratic, than systemic and realizational differences; however, such differences can cause major problems for mutual intelligibility between speakers of different dialects.

We have now begun to note some differences between accents and dialects, in a way which allows us more insight into the nature of those differences than merely noting different pronunciations, and which shows the extent to which theoretical considerations play a part in our analyses. While it is informative to note that speakers in the North of England pronounce words like *bus* as [bʊs] and that LE speakers pronounce words like *say* as [saɪ], or to note that some speakers utter an [ɹ] in some contexts rather than others, what we have done here is to say a little more than just that: we have sought to gain some insight into the nature of the phonological knowledge possessed by speakers of different accents.

Notes

1 This is not to deny that social attitudes to accents affect accent variation itself. Clearly, if we are investigating the way people speak, and if the way people speak is influenced by social attitudes to accents, then we are obliged to recognize those factors as part of the general picture.

2 Many, but not all. Some Northern accents have a distinction between /ʊ/ and /ʌ/, in which the realization of /ʌ/ is an unrounded version of [ʊ], which we might reasonably transcribe as [ɨ].

3 An alternative term would be 'contrastive difference'.

4 Many Tyneside speakers lack the /ʊ/ vs /ʌ/ distinction.

5 The term 'working-class' is vague, and enormously difficult to define. We will, none the less, assume that it is meaningful and does serve to identify what are real, if complex, differences in social class (whatever problems may reside in the vague notion 'social class' itself). The term 'London' is equally vague; none the less, it also serves a useful function, since it too allows us to identify a genuine, if hard-to-define, geographical, and perhaps cultural, entity.

6 Clearly, if there is variation between one realization and the other, and this is not noted by linguists, then a contrast that might have been wrongly taken to have been merged could re-emerge. Additionally, a contrast may merge in some phonetic environments, but not in others, leaving some minimal pairs intact while collapsing others. See 11.4 below on lexical incidence.

7 We are assuming here that LE and RP have a common source, and that LE has innovated historically in its realizations of these phonemes in particular in a way which RP has not. This assumption happens to be justified in this case, but it must not be assumed that all cases are like this. There are cases in which it is RP which has innovated. Such is the case with the /ʌ/ vs /ʊ/ contrast, which is a Southern innovation: the Northern accents have not undergone that innovation.

8 By 'vowel system' here, we mean 'system of monophthongs', ignoring diphthongs. Generally speaking, monophthongs are 'more basic' than diphthongs, but diphthongs are common, and the most common in the world's languages are the [ai]-type and [au]-type diphthongs.

Exercise

Examine the two transcriptions (A and B) of the passage given below. B is a transcription of a speaker with an RP accent, whereas A is a transcription of a speaker with another accent of English. Where you note a difference between the accents, try to say whether it is a *systemic* or a *realizational* difference. Try to *justify* your decision with appropriate evidence (from the transcriptions) and argumentation.

Since this is an exercise, and not a piece of empirical fieldwork, the sample is necessarily small. You *must*, therefore, take it to be *representative* of the accent in question.

The passage

He was bored with her talk of books on solar power. But he thought she fought well on the board and he liked her face, her eyes, and the sound of her voice. She loved ten pin bowling as well, but their first couple of games were short. He was happy in her apartment.

The transcriptions

A. [iwəz'bɔːɹdwɪðəɹ'tʰɔkə'bʉksɒn'soɫəɹ'pʰʌʊəɹ ‖ bəʔi'θɔʔʃi'fɔʔ
    wɛɫənðə'bɔːɹdəni'ɫʌɪktəɹ'fes ‖ əɹɑːɪz ‖ ənðə'sʌʊndəvəɹ'vɔɪs ‖ ʃi'ɫʌv
    'tʰɛmpɪm'boɫɪnəz'wɛɫ ‖ bəʔðɛɹ'fʌɹs'kʰʌpɫə'gemzwəɹ'ʃɔːɹʔ ‖ iwəz
    'hʉpeɪnəɹə'pʰɐɹʔmən?]

B. [iwəz'bɔːdwɪðə'tʰɔːkə'bʊksɒn'soʊlə'pʰaʊə ‖ bəti'θɔːʔʃi'fɔːʔ
    'wɛləndə'bɔːdəni'laɪktə'feɪs ‖ əɹaɪz ‖ ənðə'saʊndəvə'vɔɪs ‖ ʃi'lʌv
    'tʰɛmpɪm'boʊlɪnəz'wɛɫ ‖ bəʔðə'fɜːs'kʰʌpɫə'geɪmzwə'ʃɔːt ‖ iwəz
    'hæpiɪnəɹə'pʰɑːtmənt]

Note 1. Primary stress is indicated by means of the diacritic <'>, as in ['hæpi].
Note 2. Pause is indicated by means of the following symbol: < ‖ >.

Appendix

An Outline *of* Some Accents *of* English

1 General Australian English

Defining the General Australian English Accent

Descriptions of Australian English often distinguish between three socially defined varieties: Cultivated, General and Broad Australian. We do not examine the differences between these, which mostly concern vowel articulations. We will, however, give a brief overview of General Australian, which is spoken throughout Australia. General Australian English pronunciation has its origins in the speech of early nineteenth-century working-class speakers from the South East of England, and is therefore similar to present-day London English in some respects.

General Australian Vowels

The main characterizing properties of General Australian are to be found in vowel articulations. The vowel system of General Australian is parallel to that of RP, but with many major realizational differences, mostly of a 'vowel shift' nature, as we noted earlier in chapter 11.

The /i:/, /eɪ/, /aɪ/, /ɔɪ/ vowel shift
We described this vowel shift in chapter 11. It can be depicted as follows:

/iː/   /eɪ/   /aɪ/   /ɔɪ/
| | | |
[ɪi]   [ɐɪ]   [ɒɪ]   [ɔɪ]

The /uː/, /oʊ/, /aʊ/ vowel shift

Like the high front unrounded phoneme /iː/, the high back rounded vowel phoneme /uː/ has diphthongized, often resulting in a diphthong with a high front unrounded starting point and a high back unrounded finishing point; we will transcribe this as [ɪɯ]. This realization potentially encroaches on the space of the [əʊ]-type realizations of /oʊ/, which have shifted to [ɐʉ], with a low central unrounded starting point and a high central rounded end point, thus entering the space of /aʊ/, whose realization has shifted to [æo], in which the starting point is more front than that of [ɐʉ], and the end point lower and further back. This set of shifts can be depicted as follows:

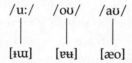

/uː/   /oʊ/   /aʊ/
| | |
[ɪɯ]   [ɐʉ]   [æo]

The /ʌ/, /æ/, /ɛ/, /ɪ/ vowel shift

A vowel shift has also affected the short vowels /ʌ/, /æ/, /ɛ/ and /ɪ/, with /ʌ/ being realized as a low front articulation in the [a] area, close to the space of the /æ/ phoneme, which is realized as [ɛ]-like. In turn, /ɛ/ is realized as [e]-like, and thus close to the space of /ɪ/, which is rather [i]-like. This articulation is, of course, distinct from that of /iː/, which, as we have seen, is diphthongal. We may depict this set of vowel shifts as follows:

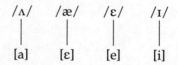

/ʌ/   /æ/   /ɛ/   /ɪ/
| | | |
[a]   [ɛ]   [e]   [i]

The /ɑː/ vs /ʌ/ distinction

The General Australian realization of /ɑː/, like that of /ʌ/, is also fronted, but the distinction between the two is not merged, since there is a length difference between them, as in [pʰat] (*putt*) vs [pʰaːt] (*part*).

General Australian Consonants

We have already noted that General Australian, like SSE, has dark l in all positions; the precise nature of the 'darkness' may entail, in both cases, retraction and lowering of the tongue body, rather than velarization as such.

General Australian is non-rhotic. It also has a process rather similar to that of Flapping in North American English: a /t/ will often be realized as a voiced articulation between vowels.

2 London English

Defining the London English Accent

By 'London English' we mean the vernacular London accent. There are more and less broad varieties of this accent, ranging from Cockney at one end of the spectrum to accents which are closer to RP in some respects at the other end.

London English Vowels

Let us postulate that the vowel system of LE is exactly parallel to that of RP, but with many major realizational differences, mostly of a 'vowel shift' nature, as discussed earlier in chapter 11.

Realizations of /ʌ/, /æ/, /ɛ/ and /eɪ/
In LE, the /ʌ/ phoneme is often realized as a short [a]-type sound. This then encroaches upon the /æ/ phoneme, which is often realized closer to [ɛ]. That in turn encroaches on the /ɛ/ phoneme, which in turn is often realized as a diphthong close to [eɪ], and that realization in turn encroaches on the perceptual space of /eɪ/. As we have seen, the /eɪ/, /aɪ/ and /ɔɪ/ phonemes also participate in this vowel shift, which we may depict as follows:

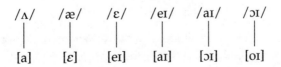

151

Realizations of /aʊ/, /ʌ/, /æ/ and /ɑ:/

Additionally, in the Cockney version of LE, the /aʊ/ phoneme is often realized as a long [a:], as in *sound* ([sa:nd])[1] and *pout* ([pa:t]). Since this vowel is distinct from the realizations of both /ʌ/ (as in *putt*: [pat]) and /æ/ (as in *pat*: [pɛt]), the distinction between the three phonemes is preserved. Note too that, since the realization of /ɑ:/ in LE has not shifted, there is a clear difference in vowel quality between it and the [a:] realization of /aʊ/.

Realizations of /ɔ:/ and /oʊ/

/ɔ:/ is typically realized as [ɔə] in open syllables (as in *war*: [wɔə]) and [oʊ] elsewhere (as in *short*: [ʃoʊʔ]). This means that one of the realizations of this phoneme encroaches upon the space of the /oʊ/ phoneme, leading to the possibility of phonemic overlapping. That phoneme in turn does not typically have an [oʊ] realization; rather, it tends to be realized as [ʊʊ] before a tautosyllabic /l/, and [ʌʊ] elsewhere.

Phonemic overlapping: /i:/ vs /ɪ/

The /ɪ/ phoneme is often realized as [iː] before a tautosyllabic /l/, as in *fill*: [fiːw].

Similarly, the /i:/ phoneme is often realized as [iː] before a tautosyllabic /l/, as in *feel*: [fiːw]. Thus pairs such as these are homophones in LE, but are minimal pairs in RP. Rather than concluding that LE has undergone a phonemic split, and therefore that this difference is systemic in nature, we will say that it is a matter of phonemic overlapping between the two phonemes, since, in other contexts, /i:/ retains its [i:] realization, and /ɪ/ retains its [ɪ] realization, as in *beat* and *bit*: [bi:ʔ] and [bɪʔ]. Note that, when the /l/ at the end of *feel* and *fill* is syllabified into a following onset, as in *feeling* and *filling*, the /l/ is no longer in the same syllable as the preceding vowel, which is realized in its normal way, thus: [fi:lɪn] and [fɪlɪn].

London English Consonants

LE differs from RP both in terms of the realization of consonant phonemes and, arguably, in terms of the consonant phoneme system.

Voiceless stop phonemes

The voiceless stop phonemes /p/, /t/, /k/ are often realized, before a primary stressed vowel, with heavy aspiration, and in the case of /t/ at least, often with affrication, *cup of tea*: [kʰʌʔpətsʰɹi]. Note too glottalized realizations (arguably foot-internally) and realization of /t/ as [ʔ] in a wider range of contexts than in RP. One such context is intervocalically (between vowels), as in *matter*: [mɛʔə].

/θ/ vs /f/ and /ð/ vs /v/ in Cockney

It has often been noted that RP minimal pairs such as *thin/fin* are homophones for many Cockney speakers, both being [fɪn]. Whether /θ/ may be said to be absent in Cockney depends very much on whether [θ] is uttered in *any* contexts by Cockney speakers. If one found that [f], rather than [θ], invariably turns up in all other contexts (e.g. between vowels, as in *Cathy*, and word-finally, as in *moth*), then one could reasonably conclude that Cockney speakers simply lack the contrast, and that there is a systemic difference here between Cockney and RP. As far as the /v/ vs /ð/ distinction is concerned, it is rather difficult to find many minimal pairs involving the two (*that* vs *vat* and *live/lithe* are examples). However, it has been noted that words such as *feather* and *with*, which have, respectively, intervocalic and word-final /ð/ in RP, are uttered with [v] in Cockney. It is not clear, however, that word-initial /ð/, as in *the, that, there, their, this*, etc., is uttered with [v] in Cockney; if such words are uttered with [ð], then we must say that there is a purely realizational difference here, with Cockney /ð/ realized as [v] intervocalically and word-finally.

Absence of /h/ in Cockney

It has been widely noted that RP minimal pairs such as *hair/air* are homophones in Cockney and perhaps generally in LE. Since Cockney appears to lack even word-internal [h], as in *behold*, this looks very much like a systemic difference. Further evidence that /h/ is simply absent in Cockney comes from two sources.

Firstly, we know that [æn] (or [ən]) is the phonetic form of the indefinite article which occurs before vowel-initial words in English, as in *an ear, an oar*, etc., whereas [æ] (or [ə]) is the form which occurs before consonant-initial words, as in *a boat, a house*, etc. Cockneys select [æn] (or [ən]) before words such as *house, hair*, etc., which might be taken to suggest that such words are phonologically vowel-initial in Cockney.

Secondly, evidence from the phenomenon of **hyper-correction** is rather telling. When speakers hyper-correct, they 'correct' words (try to make them approximate to what is considered the 'proper' pronunciation found in a prestige accent) which do not require correction. For instance, many speakers who would normally utter [ɪn] rather than [ɪŋ] for the suffix *-ing* may be none the less aware that [ɪŋ], rather than [ɪn], is the 'correct' pronunciation. Such speakers will often 'correct' words such as *kicking* from [kʰɪkɪn] to [kʰɪkɪŋ], but may also mistakenly 'correct' words such as *badminton* to [badmɪŋtən]. The significance of this phenomenon is that the speaker has /ɪn/ as his or her phonological form for the *-ing* morpheme, and overgeneralizes the 'correction' of his or her realizations to cases which do not even contain the *-ing* suffix. Similarly, speakers of French, who lack an /h/ phoneme, will hyper-correct their English, resulting in pronunciations such as [hɛə] for both *hair* and *air*. The problem for the French speaker is that, in the absence of an /h/ phoneme, she or he is not to know which of her or his /h/-less mental representations should have an /h/ added and which not. Cockney speakers have been observed to behave in just the same way as French speakers, hyper-correcting *air* to [hɛə], *ear* to [hiə] and so on. This strongly suggests that Cockney speakers, like French speakers, simply do not have an /h/ phoneme.

3 New York City English

Defining the New York City English Accent

The New York City English accent is fairly sharply defined in geographical terms, being largely confined to the boroughs of New York City (henceforth: New York). There is, however, considerable socially determined variation within New York, and this variation has been the subject of a good deal of sociolinguistic study. The New York accent is widely recognized in the United States and, like many urban accents, evokes mainly negative reactions. One of the questions addressed in the sociolinguistic studies conducted in New York is that of rhoticity. It seems clear that the accent has made the historical transition from rhotic to non-rhotic, since it has (most of) the set of diphthongs ending in schwa which are characteristic of non-rhotic accents. However, there is considerable sociolinguistic variation with respect to rhoticity, and it appears that [ɹ] in coda position is staging a comeback. Recall that the standard accent in the United States, General American, is rhotic, and that rhoticity is regarded as more prestigious than non-rhoticity.

New York City Vowels

The [ɜɪ] vowel
The [ɜɪ] realization of the /ɜ:/ phoneme, as in [pʰɜɪsənəl] (*personal*), is widely regarded as characteristic of New York speech, and is often said to characterize 'the Brooklyn accent' (although, as we noted earlier, it is by no means restricted to Brooklyn). This realization occurs before a coda consonant, so that it does not occur in *purr*. Some speakers have as well an [ɜɪ] realization of the /ɔɪ/ phoneme, also before a coda consonant, so that some minimal pairs have become homophones, as in *voice* and *verse*.

Allophones of the /æ/ phoneme
There are variable [ɛ:ə] and [æ:] realizations of /æ/ in certain environments, namely before a voiceless fricative, voiced stop or nasal when they occur in a word-final coda (although /ŋ/ behaves variably), as in *hash, past, bad, stabs, man* and *damp* but not in *pal*, with a final /l/, or *hat*, with a final voiceless stop. These diphthongal or long realizations are sometimes referred to as 'tense' realizations of the phoneme. It is not clear why these specific consonants in that position should trigger this tensing process.[2] There is considerable sociolinguistic variation in the exact phonetic form of the allophones, and, for some speakers, the [ɛ:ə] realization merges with realizations of the /ɛə/ phoneme, collapsing minimal pairs such as *bad/bared*.

Realizations of /ɔ/
New York speakers often have [ɔə] and [oə] realizations of the /ɔ/ phoneme, as in [pʰɔə] (*paw/pour/pore*), and, with an even higher

starting point, [ʊə], thus creating the possibility of partial merger with the /ʊə/ phoneme.

New York City Consonants

Rhoticity and non-rhoticity
The discussion above shows that New York speech has undergone the transition from rhoticity to non-rhoticity, and is reverting, for many speakers, to rhoticity. This phenomenon may well be resulting in greater occurrence of intrusive [ɹ], since a speaker who has been non-rhotic but is attempting to be rhotic may well insert intrusive [ɹ]s as part of a general strategy to utter [ɹ] where it may otherwise be absent.

Realizations of /θ/ and /ð/
The phonemes /θ/ and /ð/ are often realized as either affricates ([t̪θ] and [d̪ð]) or dental stops: [t̪] and [d̪]; the variation is sociolinguistically determined. Note that, for speakers who have dental stops, the phonemic distinction between alveolar and dental stops is maintained, as in [t̪ɪn] (*thin*) vs [tɪn] (*tin*). To many speakers of other varieties of English, the distinction may well be difficult to notice.

Realizations of /t/
New York speech, like General American, has Flapping of /t/ in intervocalic environments (where the first vowel is stressed), but it also has glottal stop realizations of /t/ in coda position on a greater scale than in General American. The /t/ phoneme is often heavily aspirated, to the point, at times, of being affricated, in syllable-initial position, as in [tsɪn] (*tin*).

4   Scottish Standard English

Defining the Scottish Standard English Accent

SSE is the standard accent which many Scots speak when speaking the Standard English dialect.

Scottish Standard English Vowels

A major characteristic of SSE is that there is little evidence of phonemic vowel length, but considerable evidence for allophonic vowel length. As we have seen, many of the vowel phonemes have long allophones morpheme-finally or before voiced continuants, yielding long/short allophonic differences such as [ɫif]/[ɫiːv] (*leaf/leave*).

The set of vowels which undergo the Scottish vowel length process varies from accent to accent; but /i/ and /u/ seem to undergo it in nearly all accents. In SSE, /i/, /u/, /e/, /o/, /ɔ/ and /aɪ/ appear to participate.

The /ʊ/ vs /uː/ and /ʊ/ vs /ʌ/ distinctions

One of the major systemic differences between RP and SSE is that SSE does not have the *pool/pull* (or /uː/ vs /ʊ/) type of distinction. Since SSE does not have phonemically long vowels, there is no /uː/ or /ʊ/; instead, there is a single phoneme: /u/. This is realized as long [ʉː] in the Scottish vowel-length contexts, and realized as short [ʉ] elsewhere. In Scottish accents other than SSE, the realization of this vowel can be even more fronted than the central [ʉ], sometimes approaching a French-type [y] sound (a high front rounded vowel).

SSE, unlike many North of England accents, *does* have the *put/ putt* (or /ʌ/ vs /ʊ/) type of distinction; the /ʌ/ phoneme is realized as a vowel which is rather similar to the [ʌ] of RP. Its realization is consistently distinct from the realizations of /u/. The words *put, putt, pool* and *pull* are therefore realized as [pʰʉt] (put), [pʰʌt] (putt) and [pʰʉɫ] (pull/pool), with words like *poor* realized as [pʰʉːɹ], with a long vowel.

Absence of the /ɔː/ vs /ɒ/ contrast

Another major systemic difference between RP and SSE lies in the fact that the /ɔː/ vs /ɒ/ contrast is missing in SSE, which has instead a single phoneme: /ɔ/. This means that, for many SSE speakers, RP minimal pairs such as *cot/caught* and *not/nought* are homophones. The picture is complicated by the fact that, for many SSE speakers, /ɔ/ undergoes the Scottish vowel length generalization, so that, while *not* has a short vowel, *nor* has a long vowel: [nɔːɹ].

Absence of the /æ/ vs /ɑ:/ distinction
Another striking systemic difference between RP and SSE lies in the fact that SSE does not have the /æ/ vs /ɑ:/ distinction. Instead, it has a single phoneme: /ɐ/. This is realized as a low unrounded central vowel, [ɐ], which typically does not undergo the Scottish vowel length process.

The /eɪ/ and /ou/-type phonemes
The SSE equivalent of the RP /eɪ/ phoneme is /e/, realized as long monophthongal [e:] in the Scottish vowel length contexts, and as short [e] elsewhere, as in [bet] (*bait*) and [be:ɹ] (*bare*).

The SSE equivalent of the RP /ou/ phoneme is /o/, realized as long monophthongal [o:] in the Scottish vowel length contexts, and short [o] elsewhere, as in [bot] (*boat*) and [bo:ɹ] (*boar/bore*).

The diphthongs
The SSE /aɪ/ diphthong undergoes the Scottish vowel length process, being realized as [ɐ:ɪ] in the vowel length contexts and [ʌɪ] elsewhere. The SSE /au/ diphthong is realized as [ʌu].

/ə/, /ʌ/ and /e/
Many words which, in RP, have word-final schwa and did not historically end in an /ɹ/, such as *cinema, comma, America*, are uttered with an [ʌ]-type vowel. Where RP word-final schwa was historically followed by an /ɹ/, SSE retains the /ɹ/ and has either a schwa or an /ɪ/, as in *better* and *seller*.

The short /i/ vowel found, in RP and many other accents, at the ends of words such as *very, happy, lucky* is usually an /e/ in SSE.

Scottish Standard English Consonants

Rhoticity
SSE is rhotic; the SSE /ɹ/ phoneme is typically realized as [ɹ], sometimes as [ɾ], and very rarely as [r].

The /ʍ/ vs /w/ distinction
The /ʍ/ vs /w/ distinction, as in *witch/which, weals/wheels* and *watt/what*, as the spelling suggests, is a distinction which has been

largely lost in RP, but is still present in SSE and some other British and American accents. The /ʍ/ phoneme is realized as a voiceless bilabial fricative, with a secondary velar articulation.

The /h/ vs /x/ vs /k/ distinctions
The /x/ phoneme is realized as a voiceless velar fricative ([x]) in rhymes, after low vowels and back vowels, as in *loch*. It is realized as a voiceless palatal fricative ([ç]) in rhymes, after high front vowels, as in *nicht (night)*. As with /ʍ/, the /x/ phoneme has been lost in RP; RP speakers often utter [k] instead. Unlike many accents in England, SSE speakers do not elide the /h/ phoneme before stressed vowels.

Dark 'l'
The SSE /l/ phoneme is realized as a 'dark l', i.e. [ɫ], in all contexts.

5 Tyneside English

Defining the Tyneside English Accent

By 'the Tyneside English accent' (otherwise known as 'the Geordie accent'), we mean the accent spoken by the natives of the urban areas to the north and south of the last few miles of the River Tyne before it meets the North Sea, including, principally, Newcastle upon Tyne to the north of the river and Gateshead to the south.

Tyneside English Vowels

/ʊ/ vs /ʌ/
Most Tyneside speakers are typically Northern in having no /ʊ/ vs /ʌ/ distinction: they have the former phoneme, but not the latter.[3]

/iː/
This sometimes has a diphthongal [ei]-type realization in word-final position.

/e/ and /o/
The Tyneside equivalents of RP /eɪ/ and /oʊ/ are /e/ and /o/. The Tyneside /e/ phoneme is realized, in the speech of many

Tyneside speakers, as a long monophthong: [e:]. This realization varies with a diphthongal realization ending in schwa: [e:ə]. The Tyneside /o/ phoneme may also be realized as a long monophthong by many speakers: [o:]. For some speakers the realization is a long monophthong which is a fronted [o:], of the [ø:] sort.

/ɔː/, /ɜː/ *and non-rhoticity*

Tyneside is non-rhotic and this has, of course, affected the development of the vowel system. Some Tyneside speakers lack a contrast between /ɔː/ and /ɜː/ in certain words (those which have /ɔː/ in RP and historically had an 'r' sound following the vowel), so that pairs such as *work* and *walk* are homophones: [wɔ:k]. Speakers with a 'broader' Tyneside accent maintain the distinction between /ɔː/ and /ɜː/ in words like *walk* (those which have /ɔː/ in RP but did not have a post-vocalic 'r' historically), so that /ɔː/ is realized as [ɐ:] and /ɜː/ realized as [ɔ:]: [wɐ:k] (*walk*) vs [wɔ:k] (*work*).

Schwa and non-rhoticity

The Tyneside /ɪə/ phoneme is typically realized as [ɪʌ] or [ɪɐ]. The same kind of effect occurs in realizations of /ʊə/, as in *poor*: [pʰʊɐ]. The Tyneside /ɛə/ phoneme is typically realized as a long monophthong: [ɛ:].

In Tyneside, the schwa phoneme (/ə/) can be rather [ʌ]- or [ɐ]-like (i.e. a low central unrounded vowel), but this depends on the history of the word. Where schwa was followed by an /r/ historically, it tends to be [ʌ] or [ɐ], as in *dresser*. Where this was not the case, it is [ə], as in *about*.

Low unrounded vowels

The Tyneside /æ/ phoneme is typically realized as [a], but often realized as a long [ɐ:] when it is followed by a voiced word-final consonant, as in *lad* ([lʲɐ:d]), but not in *lass* ([lʲɐs]).

/ɑː/

Although Tyneside speakers, like many Northern speakers, often have /æ/ rather than /ɑː/ in some words (e.g. *bath*), this reflects neither a systemic nor a realizational difference between Tyneside and RP. It is a lexical-distributional difference: a matter of which of the two phonemes appears in a given word.

/aɪ/ realizations
Although subject to variation (both lexical and sociolinguistic), /aɪ/ is often realized as [aɪ] or [eɪ] word-finally and before voiced fricatives, but realized with a more central starting point, as [ʌɪ], elsewhere. The effect is similar to that of the Scottish vowel length generalization on /aɪ/ in SSE.

Tyneside English Consonants

/h/ and /l/ in Tyneside
Although almost every accent of English allows for non-realization of /h/ in unstressed words (*he, him*, etc.), only some allow for non-realization of /h/ in stressed syllables. These accents can be found in many parts of England, but not in Tyneside: /h/ is almost always realized in stressed syllables in Tyneside.

Tyneside /l/ is realized as a 'clear l' in all positions.

Glottal stop and glottalisation of /p/, /t/ and /k/
The voiceless stops /p/, /t/ and /k/ often undergo glottalization between vowels, particularly when the first vowel has primary or secondary stress, as in *clipper, fitter, hacker*. The resulting realization can be transcribed as [ʔp], [ʔt], [ʔk]. Sonorants may intervene between the vowels and the stop, as in *grumpy, auntie, hankie*.

In the words cited here, we could define the context for this glottalization as foot-internal (i.e. between a primary or secondary stressed vowel and an unstressed vowel), so that /p/, /t/ and /k/ are aspirated at the beginning of a stressed syllable but glottalized if they occur foot-internally.

The 'r' realizations of /t/
Tyneside, like many Northern accents, has a realization of /t/ which is either an [ɹ]-type or an [ɾ]-type articulation. It is not entirely clear whether there is a stateable context in which this occurs, or whether there is simply a stock of words, or even phrases, in which it typically occurs. The phenomenon is probably sociolinguistically variable. The realization is reminiscent of Flapping in GA, in that it seems to occur intervocalically, but the Tyneside phenomenon is lexically much more sporadic. Typical cases seem to involve a word-final /t/ preceded

by a short vowel and followed by a word beginning with a vowel, as in *got a light, get off, put it down, but he does, shut up*. It can, however, occur word-internally, as in *better*, and after long vowels, as in *I thought he did*. The 'r' realization also seems to vary with the glottal and glottalized realizations, so that a given pronunciation of, say, *get off* can have [t], [ʔ], [ʔt] or [ɹ] as the realization of the /t/ in *get*.

6 An Overview of Some Common Phenomena Found in Accent Variation

It is clear from our brief description of the above varieties of spoken English that the speech of any speech community, and indeed of a given speaker within a community, is typically variable. It is such variation that can eventually lead to divergence between the speech of different communities over time. Several different factors are involved in such variation. A host of sociolinguistic factors is relevant. These may include the sex, age or social class of the speaker, the speaker's social aspirations, the structure of the society in which the speaker lives, and complex aspects of the social networks in which the speaker lives, involving such things as solidarity, group identity and individual identity. We have not examined these factors here, but we note that an understanding of them is vital if we are to gain a comprehensive understanding of variation in pronunciation in a given speech community.

Variation in pronunciation is also constrained by factors other than societal ones, such as the nature of the vocal tract, the relationship between the phonemes within a phoneme system, and factors to do with the relative perceptual salience of sounds, depending on what sounds they are preceded or followed by, where they occur within syllable structure, and whether they occur in stressed or unstressed syllables. The following is a summing up of the sorts of phenomena we have discussed in describing accent variation.

Vowel Phenomena

Diphthongization
Diphthongal realizations of vowel phonemes may be triggered by an adjacent consonant, as in the [iːə] realization of /iː/ before dark

l, or may occur 'spontaneously'; we have seen many examples of the latter in General American, New York City English, General Australian, London English, RP and Tyneside English.

Monophthongization
We have seen many examples of monophthongal realizations of diphthongs, as in [ɛ:] instead of [ɛə] and [ɔ:] instead of [ʊə] in RP.

Splits
As we have seen, phonemes may have allophones, but those allophones may gain phonemic status if a pattern of complementary distribution is disrupted, resulting in a newly emergent pattern of parallel distribution. Examples include the emergence of the /ə/-ending diphthong phonemes, and the /ʌ/ vs /ʊ/ distinction in RP.

Mergers
Since articulations may shift, it is possible for the realizations of one phoneme to merge with those of another, resulting in the loss of a phonemic distinction. Examples include the merging of the /ɔ:/ vs /ɑ/ distinction in parts of Canada, Utah, Nevada and Pennsylvania.

Vowel shifts
Where a merger is 'threatened' by the encroachment of the realizations of one vowel phoneme on that of another, 'evasive action' may be taken, so that the phonemic contrast is sustained. We have seen examples of this in both London English and General Australian.

Vowel reduction
Vowels frequently reduce to either a weak form (e.g. /i:/ → [i] and /u:/ → [u]), or to schwa, in unstressed syllables which, as we have seen, are perceptually less salient. This phenomenon occurs in almost every variety of English.

Consonant Phenomena

Weakening of consonants
A common phenomenon is intervocalic weakening, in which a consonant articulation becomes more vowel-like, in the sense of

becoming voiced, or undergoing a diminution in degree or duration of stricture. Flapping in North American English, voicing of /t/ in General Australian and 't-to-r' in Tyneside are all examples of this phenomenon.

In coda position, consonants often undergo weakening in the form of reduction in degree of stricture, sometimes leading to complete elision. Examples are the erosion and eventual loss of [ɹ] in non-rhotic accents, and the reduction of voiceless stops to glottal stop, which occurs to some extent in all of the accents we have considered. Vocalization of coda /l/, which occurs in London English, is another such process.

Affrication of stops

This phenomenon, in which /p/, /t/ and /k/ may be realized as [pɸ]/[pf], [tθ]/[ts] and [kx] respectively, appears to be connected with strong aspiration. It has been attested in New York City, Liverpool and London.

The principal point to be borne in mind about such processes is that they are rarely limited to specific accents of English. Nor are they limited to English. Because they arise from the nature of the human vocal tract, human perceptual capacities and the structure of human language phonologies, they are widely attested across the world's languages.

Notes

1 There is often quite marked nasalization of the vowel in cases like these, where a nasal follows an open vowel.
2 It has often been noted that auxiliary verbs which end with a tensing coda consonant, such as *can* and *had*, nevertheless do not undergo tensing.
3 Some Tyneside speakers do in fact have a contrast, between [ʊ] and an unrounded, sometimes centralized, version of [ʊ], which we might transcribe as [ɨ].

Suggested Further Reading

For a more detailed account of articulatory phonetics, see D. Abercrombie (1967) *Elements of General Phonetics*, Edinburgh: Edinburgh University Press, and J. C. Catford (1988) *A Practical Course in Phonetics*, Oxford: Clarendon Press. An introduction to phonetics which concentrates mostly on English is J. D. O'Connor's *Phonetics*, London: Penguin. For an introduction to phonetics geared towards English, and with a good introductory coverage of acoustic phonetics, see P. Ladefoged (1982) *A Course in Phonetics* (second edition), New York: Harcourt Brace Jovanovich. For standard descriptions of the RP accent, see A. C. Gimson (1993) *An Introduction to the Pronunciation of English*, London: Arnold (third edition, ed. by A. Cruttenden).

For an introduction to English phonetics and phonology which covers, in much greater detail, almost everything we have covered here, and more, see H. Giegerich (1992) *English Phonology: An Introduction*, Cambridge: Cambridge University Press. See too C. W. Kreidler (1989) *The Pronunciation of English*, Oxford: Blackwell and P. Roach (1983) *English Phonetics and Phonology: A Practical Course*, Cambridge: Cambridge University Press, which is designed largely for non-native speakers of English.

For an introduction to phonetics and phonology which focuses mostly on data from English, see M. Davenport and S. J. Hannahs (1998) *Introducing Phonetics and Phonology*, London: Arnold. For an introduction to phonological theory extending beyond the phonology of English, see any of the following: P. Carr (1993) *Phonology*, London: Macmillan; J. Durand (1990) *Generative and Non-Linear Phonology*, London: Longman; F. Katamba (1988) *An Introduction to Phonology*, London: Longman; R. Lass (1984) *Phonology*, Cambridge: Cambridge University Press; A. Spencer (1996) *Phonology*, Oxford: Blackwell.

Suggested Further Reading

Students may proceed from one of these textbooks to more advanced treatments of phonological theory, such as J. Goldsmith (1989) *Autosegmental and Metrical Phonology*, Oxford: Blackwell, and M. Kenstowicz (1994) *Phonology in Generative Grammar*, Oxford: Blackwell. For an approach to English phonetics and phonology from the viewpoint of the theory known as Government Phonology, with good coverage of varieties of British and American English, see J. Harris (1994) *English Sound Structure*, Oxford: Blackwell.

The very elementary and much simplified account of English word stress given here parallels those found in Giegerich (1992) and Roach (1983), as cited above. These accounts all derive from more or less the same pool of primary sources, which are too numerous to mention here. For detailed coverage, see E. Fudge (1984) *English Word Stress*, London: Allen and Unwin.

Many of the textbooks cited above do not cover intonation. Our account of some aspects of English intonation is very brief and incomplete. For more extensive coverage and more detailed, but none the less introductory, discussion of both the form and function of intonation in English, the reader is advised to consult Roach (1983; see above), which introduces the subject very clearly. For a general introduction to the study of intonation, see A. Cruttenden (1986) *Intonation*, Cambridge: Cambridge University Press. See too D. Crystal (1969) *Prosodic Systems and Intonation in English*, Cambridge: Cambridge University Press.

A useful book on British accents and dialects is A. Hughes and P. Trudgill (1987) *English Accents and Dialects* (second edition), London: Arnold. For an extensive description of the phonetics and phonology of a very wide range of English accents worldwide, see J. C. Wells's (1982) three-volume work *Accents of English*, Cambridge: Cambridge University Press. I have adopted Wells's three-way distinction between systemic, realizational and lexical-incidental differences between accents. For further textbook discussion of accent variation based on this tripartite distinction, see the relevant parts of Giegerich (1992; see above) and, of course, Wells (1982). I have followed Giegerich (1992) in comparing and contrasting SSE with RP and GA (for the simple reason that SSE is the medium in which I teach English phonetics and phonology). The reader should consult Giegerich (1992) for similar sorts of discussion.

It is as well to point out to any reader who wishes to pursue the further reading suggested here that the choice of symbols used to represent the vowel phonemes of various accents of English will almost certainly vary from one author to another. This is inevitable, since there is a necessary degree of arbitrariness built into such choices. However, the reader should not find it too demanding to work out the correspondences between the symbols.

Index

Index

inflectional suffix, 93
intonation, 127–32
  attitudinal function, 130–1
  fall, 128
  fall-rise, 128
  level, 128
  rise, 128
  rise-fall, 131
  syntactic function, 131–2
  tone groups, 129
  tonic syllable, 130
'intrusive r', 119–27

labial-velar, 10
labio-dental, 3
larynx, 1
lenition, 118
lexical distribution of phonemes, 145–6
light syllable, 76, 90–2
'linking r', 119–27
London English, 151–4
long vs short, 24
l vocalization, 74–5

manner of articulation, 7–10
Maximal Onset Principle, 73–6
mininal pairs, 39
monophthong, 30
monophthongization, 163
monosyllabic, 68
morpheme, 55
morphological complexity, 55

nasal assimilation, 16, 56–60, 64–5
nasal cavity, 1, 15
nasal stops (nasals), 15, 17 n. 4
natural class, 123
New York City English, 154–6
nucleus, 67
  branching nucleus, 70

onset, 66
  branching onset, 69
  empty onset, 68

open approximation, 9
oral cavity, 1

palatal, 5
palatalization, 14
palato-alveolar, 4
parallel distribution, 39, 41
perceptual and articulatory space, 141–5
phoneme, 38
phonemic merger, 140, 163
phonemic overlapping, 59–60, 64–5, 152
phonemic principle, 41
phonemic split, 82, 163
phonemic vs allophonic distinctions, 40–5
phonetic motivation, 61
phonetic similarity, 38, 41
phonological constituents, 66
phonological generalization, 44
phonological rule, 44
phonotactic constraints, 76–80
phrasal stress rule, 108
pitch, 128
place of articulation, 2–6
plosives (stops), 7
polysyllabic, 68
prefix, 56
primary articulation, 14
primary stress, 87

realization, 38
realizational differences, 137–41
Received Pronunciation (RP), 23–4
resyllabification, 83–4, 123–4
retroflex, 10
rhotic vs non-rhotic, 77, 119–27, 134–5, 156, 158, 160
rhyme, 66
rhythm reversal, 109–13
root morpheme, 55
rounded/unrounded, 20
rule ordering, 62